Praise for

THE GREAT REVENUE ROBBERY

The Great Revenue Robbery is a rallying cry for a just society. Special-interest lobbying has hollowed out the tax system. Corporations and wealthy elites have shifted their wealth and income to tax havens, and the mainstream media have polluted democratic politics with a trenchantly anti-tax agenda. This book explores this attack on tax and identifies potential progressive counterattacks, for example through financial transaction taxes, environmental taxes, and tackling tax havens. As the climate and economic crises deepen, the case for progressive taxes becomes more compelling by the day. *Aux armes citoyens!*
— John Christensen, director, Tax Justice Network

Over the past thirty years the prevailing neo-liberal ideology has framed taxes as fundamentally illegitimate. In exposing this big lie, *The Great Revenue Robbery* compellingly demonstrates the crucial and varied role of taxes in a flourishing democracy. If you want to understand what went wrong in Canadian public policy and how it can be fixed, you should read this book.
— Neil Brooks, professor of tax law and co-author of
The Trouble with Billionaires

THE GREAT REVENUE ROBBERY
How to Stop the Tax Cut Scam and Save Canada

edited by Richard Swift
for Canadians for Tax Fairness

Between the Lines
Toronto

The Great Revenue Robbery: How to Stop the Tax Cut Scam and Save Canada

© 2013 Canadians for Tax Fairness

First published in 2013 by: Between the Lines
401 Richmond St. W., Studio 277
Toronto, Ontario   M5V 3A8
1-800-718-7201
www.btlbooks.com

Every reasonable effort has been made to identify copyright holders. Between the Lines would be pleased to have any errors or omissions brought to its attention.

Library and Archives Canada Cataloguing in Publication

The great revenue robbery : how to stop the tax cut scam and save Canada / Richard Swift, editor, for Canadians for Tax Fairness.

Issued also in electronic format.

ISBN 978-1-77113-103-2

1. Corporations – Taxation – Canada. 2. Rich people – Taxation – Canada. 3. Fiscal policy – Canada. 4. Taxation – Canada. I. Swift, Richard, 1946– II. Canadians for Tax Fairness

XHJ2449.G74 2013   336.200971   C2012-907740-2

Cover design by Jennifer Tiberio. Front and back cover photo by Jennifer Tiberio. The image is part of a stone frieze on the exterior of the old Toronto Stock Exchange (what is now the Design Exchange). The frieze was designed by Charles Comfort in 1937 and depicts Canadian workers and industries in a Streamline Moderne style. It became a joke on Bay Street that one top-hatted stockbroker appears to have his hand in the pocket of the worker in front of him, though Comfort denied that this was intentional.

Page preparation by Steve Izma

Printed in Canada

RECYCLED
Paper made from
recycled material
FSC® C103567

Between the Lines gratefully acknowledges assistance for its publishing activities from the Canada Council for the Arts, the Ontario Arts Council, the Government of Ontario through the Ontario Book Publishers Tax Credit program and through the Ontario Book Initiative, and the Government of Canada through the Canada Book Fund.

 Canada Council
for the Arts
Conseil des Arts
du Canada

 Canadä

 ONTARIO ARTS COUNCIL
CONSEIL DES ARTS DE L'ONTARIO
50 YEARS OF ONTARIO GOVERNMENT SUPPORT OF THE ARTS
50 ANS DE SOUTIEN DU GOUVERNEMENT DE L'ONTARIO AUX ARTS

Contents

Prologue

JAMES CLANCY

I'VE HAD IT. Enough is enough.

So-called experts are saying that the benefits of a radical free market agenda will trickle down to regular families.

Meanwhile, the wealth and income in this country are increasingly concentrated in the hands of the top 1 per cent, household debt is at an all-time high, poverty is at unacceptable levels, and the gap between rich and poor is an absolute canyon. Corporate executives are paying themselves multimillion-dollar salaries and bonuses while exploiting tax loopholes, and bankers are being bailed out with our tax dollars.

Meanwhile, millions of Canadians are working harder and longer but haven't seen a pay hike (when you include inflation) for decades, and they're getting the humanity hammered out of them by ruthless multinational corporations with an insatiable appetite for profits. Out-of-touch politicians are spending billions on corporate tax cuts, stealth fighter jets, and American-style federal mega-prisons.

Meanwhile, the same politicians are slashing spending on public services that families need, such as health care, education, and social services, and they're making it harder to get Employment Insurance and Old Age Security benefits. Right-wing pundits on TV and AM talk radio are telling us that global warming and climate change are not serious problems and expressing open contempt for all environmental regulations.

Meanwhile, glaciers are melting, polar ice is receding, sea levels are rising, and we're experiencing more extreme weather events like forest fires, droughts, coastal floods, water shortages, and insect infestations that are killing millions of hectares of trees.

What gives me hope is that I know there are lots of folks out there who have had enough with the direction our country is headed. Our job is to harness that frustration and dissatisfaction and turn it into action.

That's where this book is going to help. What you have in your hands is a playbook for taking back our country. And it all starts with the issue of taxes.

Our economy, society, and environment are in rough shape today because right-wing wrecking crews have been dismantling every progressive brick of our tax system: cutting personal income taxes for the wealthy, cutting taxes for profitable corporations, and cutting capital gains taxes for the super-rich, to name a few examples.

The goal of the rich is to ensure that private wealth always trumps common wealth. They know that the government (its social programs, regulations, and public institutions) stands in their way. So their strategy is to destroy the government's effectiveness.

They know the best way to do that is to choke off government revenues that come from taxes. Less tax revenue means less government, and who cares if that means a less sustainable and equitable economy, society, and environment, as long as it means more private wealth for the top 1 per cent? That's all that matters to them.

Today, the common good of Canada requires, above everything else, a better, bolder, and fairer tax system.

For progressives like you and me, taking back our country starts with taking back the political debate and public narrative on taxes. This book will help you lead the fight to take back our country, in three ways.

First, it provides lots of logic, facts, and analysis on specific tax issues. It provides fresh ideas about how tax reform can help tackle the big issues facing our country today – issues that include the economy, income inequality, climate change, poverty, public services, retirement security, and labour rights. In other words, it contains all the information you need to win the battle of ideas against the anti-tax crusaders.

But it's not enough just to have ideas, analysis, and facts on our side. When it comes to winning the broader public to our cause, the truth alone will not set us free.

We also need to win the battle of values and vision. That means we must develop a compelling narrative. That's the second way this book is going to help. Most Canadians make decisions about big policy issues based on their values and the identity they want for their country. The good news is that the research shows the vast majority of Canadians share progressive values and aspirations for their country. So we must develop the language and conceptual frames that invoke those values and aspirations. This book provides valuable insights on how you can communicate progressive tax policy ideas more persuasively. It provides advice on how to use words, metaphors, and frames to develop a public narrative that expresses the moral dimension of progressive tax policies.

Third, it is our hope that this book will inspire you to adopt a new attitude on the issue of taxes. The awful truth is that too many progressives are thinking and saying the following: "Our opponents have a thirty-year head start. . . . We'll be denounced as class warriors. . . . If we talk about taxes we'll lose electoral support. . . . Let's be pragmatic and aim for smaller victories on other issues."

Progressives must want to win. But we also can't be afraid to lose. We must have the courage of our convictions. The fight over taxes isn't a side issue. It's a fight between special interests and the public interest, a fight between privilege and democracy, a fight for the heart and soul of Canada.

It's us versus them. We either roll over, play dead, and let the top 1 per cent dismantle everything we believe in, or we give them a knock-'em-down-drag-'em-out fight. You know we have no choice – we have to fight. And indeed, we should relish a fight over taxes – after all, we're right and they're wrong. So we should go on the offensive and take the fight to them.

We shouldn't be afraid of being branded class warriors. Clearly, a class war is already under way. It was started by the rich and powerful, and they're winning. But let's remember that progressives have fought and won tough battles before: universal health care; public education; a woman's right to choose; the minimum wage; public pensions; free trade unions; civil rights; unemployment insurance; safe workplaces; pay equity; the abolishing of child labour; affordable housing; clean air, water, and land.

All of these things have improved the quality of life for all Canadians. None of them were an accident. None of them happened naturally. The progressive movement said that enough is enough and fought for these things against all odds.

But we won all of those battles!

We're at the same point today with the issue of taxes. We need to dig deep and give it everything we've got. This book provides the policy ideas, communications advice, and proper attitude needed to win.

Now it's up to each one of us to take action. Don't just read this book and leave it on your shelf to gather dust. Use the insights it provides to mobilize support for our side – person by person, workplace by workplace, community by community. That's how you can help ensure that the progressive ideal of using our common wealth for the common good once again stirs Canada's collective conscience. That's how you'll help take back our country and build a better Canada for everyone.

Precious time is slipping away. This is our moment to lead. All together now!

Introduction

Tax Fairness Key to Rebuilding Canada

DENNIS HOWLETT

ANY ATTEMPT TO RESTORE responsible environmental policies, revive and expand our social programs, rebuild our crumbling infrastructure, and boost our flagging economy will be inadequate unless we also address the need to increase governments' fiscal capacity. The tax system can also play a key role in closing the gap between rich and poor – a gap that is undermining the health of our economy and threatening damage to our democracy.

Until recently, many progressive groups, including progressive political parties, have shied away from advocating for tax fairness and tax reform, fearing that the issue is political dynamite. Right wingers have encountered little opposition to their calls for deep tax cuts, especially for the rich and for corporations.

But the tide is turning. Public opinion polls tell us that faced with growing inequality and cutbacks to government programs, Canadians now strongly support tax fairness, including higher taxes on the rich and on corporations. One poll, conducted by Environics Research for the Broadbent Institute in April 2012, found that 73 per cent of Canadians support increasing the corporate tax rate and that 83 per cent support higher taxes on the rich. The same poll even found that 64 per cent of Canadians would be willing to pay "slightly higher taxes" to fight income inequality and that only 33 per cent were not willing to pay higher taxes.

Canadians for Tax Fairness was founded in 2011 by a group of visionary individuals who felt that the time had come to place the tax issue back on the agenda from a progressive point of view. This book is a collective effort to stimulate much-needed discussion about how tax policy can help rebuild our social programs, reduce the gap between rich and poor, restore environmental responsibility, and revitalize our country's democracy. The various chapters provide some context for the tax issue as well as details on a number of specific fair-tax alternatives that Canadians should seriously consider.

Tax Cuts Set the Stage for the Conservative Government's Dismantling of the Welfare State

Tax cuts have been central to Stephen Harper's strategy for dismantling what he has called the Canadian "welfare state."

Harper has long held Canada's welfare state in contempt. In 1997, when he was still a member of the National Citizens Coalition, in a speech to a meeting of the Council for National Policy, a U.S. right-wing think tank, he described Canada as "a Northern European welfare state in the worst sense of the term."[1] His views have not changed much since he became prime minister, as can be seen from the way he lectured Europeans in a speech at Davos in January 2012: "Is it a coincidence that as the veil falls on the financial crisis, it reveals beneath it, not just too much bank debt, but too much sovereign debt, too much general willingness to have standards and benefits beyond our ability, or even willingness, to pay for them?"[2]

But Harper has not had much opportunity to implement his "small government" ideology – until now.

One obstacle he faced to dismantling the Canadian welfare state was his government's minority status in its first two terms. This did not prevent his Conservative administration from chopping the recently negotiated Kelowna Accord on Aboriginal poverty and the nascent child care plan developed by his predecessor Paul Martin, but it did prevent him from making more drastic moves against established social programs.

Another obstacle was the financial and economic crisis of 2008. His Conservative government was forced to implement an economic stimulus package that boosted government spending. Downsizing government and cutting social programs on a large scale was not in the cards.

But the biggest obstacle Harper faced to realizing his dream of small government was Canadians' strong public support for social programs – especially medicare, which many Canadians view as a defining feature of their nation.

Harper was a smart enough politician to know that a direct attack on our social programs would not get him far, especially given that the federal government had been running budget surpluses for a decade by the time the Conservatives came to power.

With Ottawa enjoying a budget surplus of $13.2 billion in 2005–06, when Harper became prime minister, Canadians could see that our social programs were affordable. Indeed, it was apparent that there was fiscal room for *new* programs, such as child care and a national housing strategy. There was certainly no fiscal justification for cutting back social programs.

So Harper first had to create the political and economic context that would allow his government to move forward on its agenda to dismantle social programs. Tax cuts are much easier to sell the public than the shredding of social programs. In its first budget, in 2006, the Conservatives began implementing an ambitious tax cut plan, starting with a 1 per cent reduction in the GST. In 2008, they followed this with another 1 per cent reduction to the GST. These two cuts resulted in an annual reduction in government revenues of $12 billion.

At the same time, the Harper government announced a plan to reduce the federal corporate tax rate from 22 to 15 per cent by 2012, which would make Canada's corporate rate the lowest of any G7 country. These tax cuts would cost the government about $7.5 billion in lost revenue each year.

The Conservative government then added a number of "boutique" tax cuts to the mix. Most of these had little or no economic or social utility and were intended to appeal to specific interest groups. These included the Children's Fitness Tax Credit, the Public Transit Credit, the Tradespersons' Tool Deduction, the Textbook Amount for University Students, the Home Renovation Tax Credit, the First Time Home Buyers Tax Credit, the Volunteer Fire Fighter Tax Credit, the Children's Art Tax Credit, and the Family Caregiver Tax Credit.

The Children's Fitness Tax Credit, for example, which allowed parents to claim a nonrefundable tax credit for their children for things like hockey, dance lessons, and martial arts training, went disproportionately to upper-income families. Over 70 per cent of that benefit went to the top one-quarter of families – those with incomes over $50,000. Yet according to a University of Alberta study, that tax credit did little to encourage participation in youth sport.[3]

These boutique tax credits offered only $75 in tax savings for middle- and upper-income families, but when summed together, they cost the federal government several hundred million dollars a year in lost revenue. It is important to note that lower-income families who can't afford to pay for children's sports or whose income is below the level where they start to pay taxes have gained nothing from these tax cuts.

In 2009, as if all these tax cuts were not enough, the Conservatives introduced the Tax Free Savings Account, which allows individuals to save up to $5,000 a year without paying any tax on the interest earned. The Finance Department has estimated that this program cost the federal government $155 million in revenues in 2010.

Thus, within a few years, mostly through tax cuts, the Conservatives had given away the budget surpluses they inherited from the Liberals. As a consequence, by 2009 they were running a deficit of more than $40 billion. Between 2009 and 2010, federal tax cuts cost $34 billion in lost government revenues – 63 per cent of the deficit. The recession of 2008–09 reduced revenues and the stimulus program increased spending, yet the federal budget would have gone into deficit in any case as a result of tax cuts, even if the global economic crisis had not hit Canada in 2008.

The tax-cutting policies at the federal level were duplicated by many provincial governments. Overall, federal and provincial taxes as a share of GDP fell between 1998 and 2011 from 45 to 33 per cent.

Federal and provincial tax cuts have greatly reduced the fiscal capacity of the state and have set the stage for an assault on Canada's social programs – an assault that is only now beginning in full force.

Unnecessary and Counterproductive Austerity Is Just Beginning

The 2012 federal budget was the first real austerity budget that the Conservatives were able to bring down. It featured deep cuts to public service jobs and government services as well as major changes to Employment Insurance and pensions. It also eliminated a number of government agencies altogether.

By the time the job cuts are fully implemented, public service spending will have been reduced by $5.2 billion annually and 29,600 jobs will have been eliminated. Public service workers deliver many government programs, and cuts this deep are sure to affect the quality of these services as well as their accessibility.

The government has also announced plans to delay by two years the age at which Canadians can start receiving Old Age Security and the Guaranteed Income Supplement, from 65 to 67. This will begin to undermine the one area where Canada has been relatively successful at reducing poverty: among seniors. It will also shift the burden of supporting low-income seniors to the provinces for an additional two years.

The Harper government has also tightened the eligibility rules for Employment Insurance by requiring all recipients to accept work that is within an hour's commute from their home and that provides 70 to 90 per cent of their previous salary.

The Harper government is still reluctant to cut health care spending because of strong public support for medicare. So it has unilaterally decided – without any negotiation with provincial governments – to continue to increase federal transfers for health by 6 per cent per year until 2016–17. But it has also served notice that after that date, the increase will be reduced to either the nominal rate of economic growth or 3 per cent, whichever is greater. The impact of this policy will not be felt immediately, but in the long run, unless this policy is reversed, it will have a huge negative impact on our most cherished social program.

Departmental budgets in social welfare areas are also being cut drastically. The Conservatives plan to cut the Health, Aboriginal Affairs, and Human Resources and Skills Development departments by a total of $1.2 billion over three years.

Funding for the National Council of Welfare has been eliminated completely, along with funding for the First Nations Statistical Council and the Centres of Excellence in Women's Health.

And this may not be the end of it. Details on the full extent of planned government cuts have not been made public, and even more surprises may be in store in the next few federal budgets.

Debt and Deficits – the Wrong Diagnosis; Austerity – the Wrong Medicine

Austerity is a bitter pill to swallow, especially for those who lose their jobs or who depend on social programs. But it is even more galling for those who understand that it is the wrong medicine for our ailing economy.

To cure our economic ills, we need a good diagnosis and the right medicine. The problem with the Canadian economy is not high deficits and debt loads, but weak consumer demand and low productivity resulting from a widening gap in income distribution and from too many people who aren't able to contribute to the economy to their full potential because of poverty and unemployment.

Federal and provincial deficits are not that serious a problem, and creative ways can to be found to address them, but we need to understand where those deficits have come from if we are going to develop the right fixes.

There are three main reasons for high government deficits in Canada:

1. Tax cuts.
2. The recession of 2008–09, which reduced tax revenues and required extra spending on economic stimulus measures.
3. A very slow and shaky economic recovery with continuing high levels of unemployment.

Government overspending is not causing the deficits. Government spending as a share of the economy has actually been going down.

We need to lower deficits by fixing the revenue problem, not just by cutting spending.

When deficit reduction is pursued mainly through spending cuts, especially as they relate to government services and social programs, this can further harm poor people in Canada, who have already suffered the most from a financial and economic crisis they did nothing to cause.

Relying on austerity alone to reduce deficits also risks increasing unemployment and poverty in Canada. This in turn could push Canada into another recession, further reducing tax revenues and thereby undermining the chances of restoring fiscal balance. This is already happening in several European countries such as Greece and Spain.

In an Orwellian twist, the Conservative government called its 2012 omnibus budget bill the *Jobs, Growth and Long-term Prosperity Act*. Yet a Parliamentary Budget Office study released in April 2012 estimated that the aggregate employment impacts of federal and provincial cut-backs would be the loss of more than 100,000 jobs by 2015. To quote from that report: "As the drag from the restraint and reductions in government spending take hold, the unemployment rate is projected to be 0.3 percentage points higher over the period 2013 to 2015 than would otherwise be the case." The budget cuts will also have a negative impact on GDP growth. The PBO estimates that "on a cumulative basis over 2012 to 2017, the output gap is over 50 per cent larger than would be the case without the restraint and reductions in government spending on programs."[4]

The underlying weakness of consumer spending is due in large part to the widening gap between rich and poor. Wealth has become far too concentrated in the top 10 per cent or even 1 per cent. At the same time, middle- and lower-income Canadians have seen their incomes stagnate or decline. Many middle- and lower-income Canadians have tried to extend their purchasing power by taking out loans, but consumer debt is now maxed out and consumer demand has weakened. The rich just can't make up the slack, and neither can the very rich, because there are so few of them. There are only so many cars one person can use.

Giving businesses more tax breaks is not going to boost investment and job creation if those businesses are not sure they will be able to sell their products and services. What would help our economy most, and the business sector in particular, is policies to redistribute wealth and reduce unemployment. And the most effective ways to do those things would be to make taxes fairer and improve social programs.

We Need Revenue-Side Solutions

Deficit reduction strategies, if they are to succeed, require measures to increase revenue. Increasing personal income taxes on middle- and lower-income Canadians could undermine the weak economic recovery, but there are many innovative tax measures that deserve consideration. Some provinces may require broad but small progressive tax increases in order to restore a healthy fiscal balance, but at the federal level we probably do not need general tax increases.

The following are some of the key components of a tax fairness program for the federal government:

1. Raise the Corporate Tax Rate

The federal corporate tax rate has been lowered from 22 per cent in 2007 to 15 per cent today. Canada has led the race to the bottom to the point where Canada's corporate tax rate is one of the lowest in the industrialized world.

According to the PBO, the reduction in the corporate tax rate will cost the government $11.5 billion between 2011 and 2014. That is money that might otherwise have gone towards reducing the deficit or funding a national pharmacare program.

There is no evidence to support the government's claim that corporate tax cuts create jobs. Canadian companies are just sitting on their extra retained profits; foreign-owned companies are just taking more of their profits out of the country. Companies are not investing this money because they aren't sure consumers will be able to buy more products and services.

Companies would be helped more if more people found work so that they could afford to buy their products and services. They would also be helped if governments invested more in infrastructure, education, and job training – all three figure more prominently in decisions about where business invests.

Nobel Prize–winning economist Joseph Stiglitz has pointed out that each dollar of government spending on infrastructure and social programs provides more than a dollar's worth of economic stimulus, while each dollar of tax cuts provides less than fifty cents' worth of economic stimulus.[5]

According to the Alternative Federal Budget 2012, raising the corporate tax rate to 21 per cent could generate $10.5 billion a year and still ensure a level of corporate taxation competitive with that of other industrial countries.

2. Raise Taxes on High-Income Earners and Close Tax Loopholes

Canada is growing more unequal. Social and economic disparities are threatening democracy itself. The wealthiest among us are able to influence political decision making, and they are doing so in order to protect and strengthen their own interests. The wealthiest, who can afford to pay a fair share of our public service costs, enjoy a tax system that is skewed in their favour.

A more progressive tax system would reduce the gap between rich and poor and boost the economy by stimulating consumer spending among middle- and lower-income Canadians. Higher tax rates on higher income brackets should be restored.

But restoring higher income tax rates on higher incomes will not on its own ensure that the rich pay a fairer share. Most very wealthy people don't pay anything close to the highest marginal rate on their income because they find all kinds of ways – both legal and illegal – to avoid paying taxes.

One of the most unfair things about our tax system is that income from investments is taxed at a much lower rate. And the really wealthy get most of their income from investments. More than two-thirds of the capital gains exemption goes to tax filers who make more than $100,000 a year. This cost the government over $11 billion in 2007.

Governments need to adopt the principle articulated by the Carter Commission on taxation fifty years ago: "a buck is a buck," regardless of how you earn it.

Tax breaks that disproportionately benefit the rich, such as the very high limit on RRSP contributions and the Stock Option Deduction, need to be curtailed. The Stock Option Deduction, for example, saw 90 per cent of the benefit going to the less than 1 per cent of tax filers with incomes of over $250,000.

The Alternative Federal Budget 2012 estimates that these measures would increase revenue by $11.5 billion annually.

3. Implement a Financial Transactions Tax

International momentum has been building for a tax of 0.5 per cent or so on all financial market transactions, including those involving stocks, commodities, currencies, and derivatives. The resources thereby generated would be channelled toward fighting poverty and climate change at home and abroad. This would raise badly needed revenue and would also discourage the runaway speculation that was one cause of the financial crisis in 2008. It would also ensure that the financial sector, which is currently taxed at much lower rates than other sectors of the economy, pays a fair share of taxes.

The Alternative Federal Budget 2012 estimates that this tax could raise $4 billion a year in Canada.

4. Introduce a Tax on Large Estates of Inherited Wealth

Canada is one of the few countries that does not have an inheritance or estate tax. As a result, wealth is passed on from generation to generation and becomes more and more concentrated in the hands of a few. An estate tax should be applied only to amounts in excess of $5 million. This would ensure that inheritances of cottages or other property that has been held within families for decades would not be affected. Nor would there be a tax penalty for family farms that are being passed on to the next generations.

The Alternative Federal Budget 2012 estimates that such an estate tax would raise $1.5 billion a year.

5. Tackle Tax Havens

Canada needs to do more to curb tax havens and tax evasion, especially at a time when deficit cutting is threatening to gut our social programs and to undermine governments' ability to ensure food safety and environmental protection. A recent study by the Tax Justice Network estimates that Canada could be losing up to $80 billion a year to various forms of tax evasion.[6] That is more than half of all health care spending and more than twice the federal deficit. Almost a quarter of all of Canada's investment overseas is now going to known tax haven countries, according to a 2012 Statistics Canada report.[7] This amounts to over $150 billion in just one year. Much of this is being sent to tax havens to avoid paying taxes.

Going after resource extraction companies and Canadian banks, as well as many rich individuals who are taking advantage of tax havens to avoid paying taxes to Canada and to the developing countries where they are extracting resources, is a much better way to reduce the deficit than cutting spending on health, education, and environmental protection.

Canada needs to push for stronger international action. This would benefit Canada and would also help developing countries, which are now losing ten times more in illicit flows of money out of their countries than they are receiving in aid. Specifically, the Canadian government should do four things: (1) publish an estimate of the size of the tax avoidance problem in Canada, and its cost to the federal and provincial treasuries; (2) increase the resources of the international compliance division of the Canada Revenue Agency so that it can do more to catch tax cheats; (3) compel corporations to publish what they pay in taxes on a country-by-country basis; and (4) push for stronger action against tax havens at the G20 and the United Nations.

It is difficult to say how much additional revenue could be raised by curbing tax havens, for one of the main characteristics of these havens is their secrecy, which makes it difficult to make an accurate estimate. While some actions can be taken by Canada on its own, more effective regulation of tax havens will require international co-operation. Given that nearly a quarter of Canada's foreign investments are now going to tax haven countries, and assuming that in most cases this is in part to avoid paying taxes, we can safely conclude that the losses are in the tens of billions of dollars.[8]

All of these progressive tax measures together would raise about $36 billion in additional revenue, according to the Alternative Federal Budget 2012.

6. Introduce Smart and Progressive Carbon Taxes

The tax system can also be used to achieve both environmental and poverty reduction goals. One of the best ways to reduce greenhouse gases that cause climate change is through a carbon tax. These taxes are a more efficient and transparent and less corruptible way to put a price on carbon than cap-and-trade quotas. Carbon taxes also avoid the speculation, uncertainty, and unfair windfall gains associated with cap-and-trade systems. Carbon taxes send a clear price signal to businesses and consumers and in that way encourage conservation. Goods from countries that don't have similar measures can be taxed at rates that reflect the emissions associated with their production, processing, and transport. Goods from highly impoverished nations can be exempted, however. This pressures other countries to enact climate change measures and also ensures that Canada's exporters are not placed at a competitive disadvantage.

Rich people pollute more (i.e., they have a much larger ecological footprint) than those with low incomes. Emissions per person in the top quintile are almost double those in the bottom quintile.[9] High-income families find it easier than poor families to reduce their emissions by changing consumption patterns and by upgrading their homes and vehicles to be more energy efficient. Carbon taxes need to take this difference into account by providing a progressive green tax refund. This would provide a majority of Canadians with a larger annual credit than they pay out in carbon taxes.

British Columbia has had a very successful carbon tax since 2008. It has been responsible for a 15 per cent reduction in fuel consumption and for a 9.9 per cent reduction in per capita greenhouse gas emissions – the best result in all of Canada. And B.C. has achieved this without negatively affecting economic growth and has delivered on the promise of keeping the tax revenue neutral. A recent poll found strong public support for B.C.'s carbon tax: 64 per cent of respondents said it had been good for the province.[10]

7. Use the Tax System to Help Reduce Poverty and Inequality

The tax system is a powerful tool for redistributing wealth. Closing the gap between rich and poor is a moral and ethical imperative; it is also vital to restoring a healthy balance to a market-based economy. The market does not do very well at sending signals about what should be produced unless those with lower incomes have sufficient resources to create the effective demand for goods and services that meet their basic needs. When wealth becomes too strongly concentrated in the hands of a few, consumer demand weakens, with disastrous consequences for job creation and economic growth. As Linda McQuaig and Neil Brooks made clear in *The Trouble with Billionaires,* wealth concentration also undermines democracy by enabling those with great wealth to influence government policies in ways that benefit themselves to the disadvantage of the majority.

The tax system can help take an unfair share of resources from the rich and channel those resources to the poor.

The tax and transfer system has worked in the past to ameliorate the gap between rich and poor. Between 1981 and 2010, market income inequality as measured by the Gini co-efficient increased by 19.4 per cent. This was partly offset, however, by transfers and taxes so that after-tax inequality increased by only 13.5 per cent. That is still a high number, but it could have been much worse.

Our tax and transfer system could be doing a much better job. A recent study by the Centre for the Study of Living Standards found that

> if Canada's redistributive effort were to be raised to the OECD average, nearly two thirds of the increase in after-tax inequality that has taken place in Canada since 1981 would be eliminated. Equally, if the level of redistributive effort that was in place in Canada in 1994, the year where redistribution was greatest, had still been in place in 2010, one half of the rise in after-tax inequality between 1981 and 2010 would be reduced. Canada thus has much room to increase its redistributive effort. What is needed is political will.[11]

Several programs within the Canadian tax system have been highly successful in reducing poverty. Children, for example, have done well from the Canadian Child Tax Benefit, the National Benefit Supplement, and the Child Disability Benefit. In many provinces and territories, federal and provincial/territorial efforts have been combined in the National Child Benefit, to which the federal government has contributed just over $10 billion a year. In 2011 the maximum annual benefit was $3,485 for the first child to families with net incomes below $24,183. The National Child Benefit is a universal program that provides benefits even to those families whose incomes are below the level where they have to pay taxes. It delivers more support to families that need more help, but almost 90 per cent of families with children get some portion of the benefit.

The National Child Benefit is the main reason why there are fewer low-income families with children than there used to be. Between 1998, when the program was introduced, and 2005, the percentage of such families fell from 17.6 to 10.5 per cent. Child poverty could practically be eliminated if this benefit were increased to a maximum of $5,400 per child. This would cost just over $5 billion. That may seem like a lot, but it could be partly offset by eliminating the Universal Child Care Benefit, which costs about $2.5 billion a year.

The Working Income Tax Benefit, introduced in 2007 and strengthened in 2009, provides a supplement to the working poor to offset the loss of benefits resulting from going off social assistance as well as the increased costs associated with working, such as transit. It is a refundable tax credit that provides up to about $1,000 a year for single persons and about $1,750 per couple, depending on the province. The credit is slightly more for those with a disability. This benefit has provided a positive incentive for people to move off welfare and into the workforce, but it does not do enough to help working poor families who have never been on social assistance. The maximum benefits should be raised, and the program should extend its reach higher up the income ladder so that it becomes a major income support for Canadians who work but remain poor. Raising minimum wages so that a single person working full time would have an income above the poverty line would be an important complement to this program – one that would not require any government expenditure and that could actually increase tax revenue.

Old Age Security and the Guaranteed Income Supplement have helped reduce poverty among Canadian seniors to less than 5 per cent. These programs are succeeding and should not be cut back; indeed, the benefits they offer should be increased with the goal of completely eliminating poverty among seniors. It is becoming increasing important to strengthen public pensions and improve the OAS and GIS programs now that more and more Canadian workers are reaching retirement age without robust company pensions or private RRSP savings to rely on. Less than 40 per cent of Canadians are now covered by workplace pensions, and employers have been reducing benefit levels. Only 30 per cent of Canadians who are eligible to do so contribute to RRSPs, and many of those who have retirement savings have seen them shrink as a result of the global economic recession in 2008.[12]

A small part of the $29 billion that the government now spends on tax breaks for RRSPs and company pensions that mainly benefit wealthier Canadians – an amount that is more than half the total cost of the OAS – could be used to increase the OAS/GIS benefit for single seniors to at least the poverty line and keep the retirement age at 65. These government programs could be complemented by improvements to the CPP to strengthen our old age security system. A doubling of the income replacement rate from 25 per cent of covered earnings to 50 per cent of average adjusted pensionable earnings, as suggested by the Canadian Labour Congress, could be achieved through a modest increase in employee and employer contributions, with no additional cost to the government.

Conclusion

Tax cuts that mainly benefited corporations and the rich, begun in the 1990s by the Liberal governments of Jean Chrétien and Paul Martin, and taken to new depths by the Harper Conservatives, have set the stage for a wholesale assault on our social programs. Because many of the changes are being phased in over time, the impact is not yet fully apparent. Nor have all the cuts that are planned been announced. We can be sure, though, that by the time Harper has finished dismantling the "Canadian welfare state," we will not recognize Canada as the country we have known.

All is not yet lost. We can still reverse the changes that are being made. But any serious attempt at rebuilding and extending our social programs and government services, which are so vital to a healthy society, economy, and environment, will require a commitment to a policy of tax fairness in order to restore the fiscal capacity of government to serve the common good.

Opposition parties should not shy away from the tax issue. It is no longer the bogeyman it once was, because Canadians are beginning to realize that they are losing far more from government spending cuts to social programs and services than they have gained from tax cuts. There is strong support for increasing taxes on corporations and the rich; there is even a willingness to accept modest, broad-based tax increases if these will help restore and strengthen social and environmental programs. There is a growing awareness that tax policies can also help fight climate change, reduce inequality, and combat poverty, thereby addressing some of the fundamental causes of Canada's ailing economy.

We hope this book will help raise public awareness of this vital issue, stimulate much-needed debate about fair tax policy, and embolden political leaders to explain more clearly how they propose to fund the rebuilding effort that will be badly needed when the Harper government is finally replaced.

1

Passing On the Torch

TRISH HENNESSY

IN 1935, AMID THE HOPELESSNESS of the drought-scorched Prairies, my mother was born into a very stark reality.

A child of the Great Depression, she grew up in a world of uncertainty, without the staples we now consider the basics of life.

Today, the most cherished way to spend time with family and friends is to go out for a nice restaurant meal.[1] Back then, rural families had no choice but to grow and raise the food they ate. Food was a matter of survival, not entertainment.

The other word for clothes was *hand-me-downs*.

Running water, electricity, flushable indoor toilets: these were luxuries of the rich. The granite kitchen countertops that today we consider desirable middle-class renovations were the domain of kings and queens.

In my mother's time, going to the washroom meant a trip to the outhouse winter, spring, summer, or fall. Christmas was extraordinary, not just for the rare appearance of mandarin oranges (fruit!) in winter, but, more importantly, for the coveted green tissue that cradled each orange; a superior substitute for the rough pages of the Sears Roebuck catalogue.

In those days, children squeezed into one-room schoolhouses for as long as their parents could spare them from field work. Some, such as my stepfather at age six, harnessed a horse, hitched a wagon, and drove themselves to school, picking up the teacher along the way because there were no school buses and car ownership had not yet become "democratized." Children actually did trudge through a mile of snow to get to school in those days.

For them, the prospect of finishing high school was marginal because there was work to be done and, after all, the halls of higher learning were reserved for an elite few.

The notion of individual responsibility was a source of stubborn pride. But also, you needed it to survive. I could see that in my parents.

So, too, was the reality of social responsibility. At harvest time, if you were finished getting your hay off the field, you helped your neighbours with theirs. You baked a pie, a cake, or a casserole for the family whose doors had been darkened by the death of a loved one. Those who fell sick relied on the goodwill of family and friends. Universal public health care had not yet been imagined.

Shared sacrifice was a way of life. Multiple generations lived under one roof, with children sharing not just bedrooms but beds. For seniors, there were no RRSPs, retirement condos, or plans for leisurely trips. One of the best predictors of poverty was old age – Canada's public pension system had not yet been built.

Everyone was more than willing to do their part, but when the toll of the Great Depression brought about mass poverty, a movement inevitably erupted. Men who'd lost their jobs in the 1930s hopped railway cars to Ottawa, desperate for help to feed their families and angry at a government that ignored their hardship.

Those were the days before Employment Insurance, such as it is. Back then options in hard times were limited. There were soup kitchens. The government had set up "relief" camps that compensated unemployed men 20 cents a day for doing construction work in the bush. The Regina Riot erupted as a protest against those camps.

The early 1900s had been distinguished by the growth of urban areas in Canada, an emerging economy. But during the worst of the Great Depression, there was a significant reversal. Many sought refuge in rural life, investing their hopes in the land.

Progress, in all its forms, is never without struggle.

Despite the palpable hardships of the Great Depression, my mother would say she grew up in the best possible era. The Depression and the Second World War became a unifying force. My mom's generation, and her parents', understood full well that Canadians were better off acting together than they were facing life's hardships on their own. It wasn't a sacrifice but, rather, a necessity. During the Depression, people saw no option but to move forward together, as best they could.

The benefits of acting together added up. In my mother's lifetime,

Canadians built the roads, water mains, sidewalks, bridges, and sewage systems needed to service burgeoning cities. They vastly reduced the incidence of poverty among seniors, improved health outcomes and the chance to live a longer, more dignified life. Out of the Depression's dust, they created a middle class, with all the comforts that came with it.

By the time I was born in 1965, on the tail end of Canada's baby boom, the world had moved on from the stark realities of 1935. Canada was maturing into a prosperous country full of promise. Children like me benefited from a range of public incentives to do well that had never before existed in Canada's history.

It meant that a child like me – raised in a humble rural community that relied on good weather to yield a wheat crop that would pay the bills – enjoyed the luxury of choice and opportunity. We still grew and raised most of our own food. I spent many a summer back bent under a hot sun picking the weeds crowding out our annual crop of vegetables – food slated for pickling, canning, and freezing. In the fall, the cattle went to market and one ended up in our own butcher shop to keep a family of eleven fed for a year.

But as a child of the 1960s, I had the luxury of imagining a life beyond subsistence. I could gaze upon the expansive horizon of a wheat field, and within the thin fold of earth and sky I could believe in anything and everything all at once. In my case, the promise met with reality. I could be and do anything in my lifetime. That was the good fortune into which I was born.

Third-generation middle class. That's how new the middle-class lifestyle is in Canada. We sometimes forget how relatively young that promise is. We, the fortunate ones who have inherited a gift. That is, every April 30th the people who came before us paid their taxes and, as we enter adulthood, we return the favour. We do it for the seniors, who deserve a decent retirement. We do it for our children, who deserve a chance at a good public education. We do it for the unborn, for the dying, and we do it for ourselves. It was commonly accepted that taxes were the price of a civilized society but, also, a happier one.

Taxes, the gift we give each other. They're not simply a coarse monetary exchange. They fuel our most cherished public programs and, also, the ones we take for granted. City streets. Multi-lane highways. Overpasses and bridges. Sidewalks. Street lights. Sewage systems and water filtration plants. These were not glamorous pursuits, they are simply the basics of an advanced society.

Public libraries. Curbside garbage pickup. 911. Environment Canada. Food inspection. A national census. Parks. Museums to preserve our history. A public pension program that has greatly reduced poverty among seniors. The idea of a "Just Society." And, going back to the beginning, a national railway system designed to unite.

These were built by taxes.

We looked to corporate Canada to give back, too. I grew up in the days of the company picnic, but what never ended up in the community newspaper was the list of public services that corporate taxes helped fund in return for the right to do business among us. The idea of profitable corporations hiding behind the veil of mobility – the transnational corporation schmoozing its way through successions of government to shield record-high profits from the responsibility to pay taxes – was unthinkable when I was growing up.

I've learned something from the troubles of my parents and grandparents. As Canadians, we emerged from the double trauma of the Great Depression and the Second World War with fundamentally changed expectations of the world, of our government, and of one another. By the middle of the 1940s, Canadians had entered an era of infrastructure development and the growth of a social safety net that had never before existed.

We did so through the hard currency of taxation. It was considered an act of social citizenship. To be caught evading taxes was a degree of humiliation best avoided. Good citizens paid the taxes they owed.

Then what happened? Over time, we dehumanized taxation as an act of giving. We talked about *the tax man*. There were resentful quips about the only two certain things in life: death and taxes. Our politicians started talking about taxes as a burden, the one that explained that chip on our shoulder. And the notion of "relief," which in the 1930s meant helping out a brother when he needed you to spare a dime, became eclipsed by the political mantra of "tax relief," tax cuts to relieve the "burden" of "working families."

In other words, we gave in to a political culture that demonized taxes and divorced them from the gift we give each other.

Rather than an act of giving, taxes were talked about as an act of taking. The tax man was taking our money and governments were wasting it. Tax dollars were better off in your own pocket, for you to do with what you will. We elected politicians based on pronouncements such as "I never met a tax that I liked."

We stopped talking about the purchasing power of taxes. A generation of Canadians were born into a social culture that fully understood the value of bulk buying through, say, Wal-Mart or Costco, but severed that relationship when it came to thinking about the bulk purchases our taxes could fund, such as a universal pharmacare program or affordable public child care. We stopped imagining a public space funded by taxpayers collectively. We courted a return, instead, to a pre-1930s reality without remembering its bleakness.

We assumed a false sense of power by morphing into consumer citizens, far removed from the idea of social citizenship. We mistook our humanity as an entity in itself, isolated from acts of giving, unrelated to the artery of public services and infrastructure that taxes made real. We had disowned our own imprint.

Suddenly, there was no tax too big or small to dislike. Right-wing governments created bogeymen out of political leaders who called for new taxes of any kind, even ones (like carbon taxes) that could be as good for the planet as they were for ailing public coffers. Even left-wing political leaders surfed the wave, playing "against type," trying to bring down governments that looked to the hst as a solution. The fight was cast as "good" taxes versus "bad" ones, but the effect of the combined pile-on was the same: they ended up killing any taste for taxes the public ever had.

Blame the politicians for turning against the expansion of the postwar era and reducing us all to a tiny, insular social village. But what of us, those social citizens who inherited a country that once held such promise for progress, for greater equality, for a more caring and just society? What of our responsibility to keep that promise alive, to advance it in real terms?

For almost two decades, our political leaders have appealed to us as consumer first, citizen last. And we have let them. To what end? As the tally of tax cuts swells – $50 billion lost annually and counting[2] – our public world shrinks. The pool is so shallow that our political class is now bluntly going after the country's public sector workers, slashing services but, also, jobs. Pitting public sector workers against private sector ones. Citizen against citizen. *And we let them.*

What, amid the heresy of the comfort class to reject the measures our forbearers set in place for our collective wellbeing, have we overlooked? The lesson from my mother's era, that we simply cannot do it alone; that we need each other. That lesson is still hardwired into our historical memory. It is within us somewhere, ready to be tapped – perhaps anxious for it.

It may be part of the reason why the citizens of Toronto barely blinked an eye several years ago when their former mayor, David Miller, implemented a new tax on plastic bags. A simple political act, charge a nickel a bag, sparked a revolution in Toronto in terms of plastic bag use. Overnight, citizens who had probably been open to new ways to be environmentally responsible readily owned up by creating a new market for cloth bags to replace the plastic bag addiction (an addiction that developed because plastic was the only option on offer for the longest time).

Plastic bag use in Toronto has declined dramatically. Was it a crass consumerist attempt to dodge a five-cent tax? Or was it a calling to an order of higher social citizenship?

Ask Canadians, as Environics Research has, what do you do to be a good citizen? They say: Volunteer. Be kind and generous. Pay taxes.[3] Ask Canadians if they would pay higher taxes to protect social programs, and in the spring of 2012, the majority told Environics they would be willing to do so.[4] Ask Canadians if taxes are mostly good or mostly bad, and they consistently say they're good.[5] Corporations, too, have a social responsibility to contribute to the communities where they do business. We have a history of co-operative movements embedded in our collective memory.

Tax contribution as an act of social citizenship, as a measure of the public good, as virtue. The concept of virtue has been erased from the Canadian political discourse. Our political leaders have not yet caught up with citizens on this value, but our history is rich with the sensibility that governments are more than cashiers handing out cash discounts at the till; that we, the citizens of Canada, are more than consumers. Our true power is greater than the size of our individual wallets.

Former Prime Minister John Turner (1984): "The budget used to be related to taxation."[6] Back to the promise of a better life and the price Canadians are willing to pay for such happiness. What if those among us who inherited a kinder, more caring Canada approached the concept of budgets and taxation from the starting point of social citizenship, as our grandparents did? Imagine how different the conversation could be.

Canada's baby boomers, among the most affluent generation ever to have lived, benefited from a generous stretch of prosperity and from the social pact those who came before us had made implicit as a result of the Depression and world war. Over my shoulder, I see Gen Xers, Gen Ys, and more to come. I see a future in search of hope. I see the need for a renewal of our social pact, a renewed commitment to the things we do for one another and for ourselves. Taxes are inevitably at the heart of that renewal. It is a matter of fairness, of efficiency, of social responsibility.

Following the shock of the 2008 global economic meltdown, it is time to revisit these ideas about our own country and its future. Our governments fell into a state of fiscal deficit. They're intent on returning us to balance. But what is balance, aside from a line item on an accountant's sheet? Balance is you *and* me, not you *against* me. Balance is the noble pursuit of a more equitable society; the weighing of both financial and social costs.

Balance, how we achieve it, and what kind of society we could become in service of that mission – that's the discussion we, as a third-generation middle-class country, have not yet begun. It's a discussion that transcends the pugilism of partisan politics, one that goes beyond the cold numbers case, because a tax is never just a number. It's never about a particular program or service.

A tax is the gift generations of social citizens hand down, one to the next. It's our public inheritance – the one we get whether our parents were rich, poor, or middle class. It's our great equalizer. We've been doing it for a long, long time – way before Canada blossomed into one of the ten richest nations on the planet. The torch was lit by others, but it's ours to pass on.

2

Pushing the Envelope

The Overton Window and the Left

DIANA GIBSON

THE 1990s IN CANADA were a watershed for health care privatization. In 1994 the Canadian Life and Health Insurance Association (CLHIA) observed that it had typically been sending out notices that governments had added this or that benefit to their plans and that their members' insurance companies no longer needed to cover it. Then in the 1990s the CLHIA announced a "totally different economic environment": governments had stopped expanding social programs and instead had begun to cut them. The CLHIA began sending out more "cheerful" notices advising members of the delisted services that they could now offer customers. The CLHIA predicted that this was going to be a "boon" for the insurance industry. The economic agenda was changing, which heralded that good times were about to start rolling for the private health insurance industry – and more broadly, for corporations and the wealthy.

This was a profound shift. Corporate interests have not been so well served since before the New Deal in the 1930s. That decade was a turning point for corporate elites and the wealthy, for it is when Conservative Prime Minister R.B. Bennett finally followed Roosevelt's lead in the United States and introduced a Canadian version of the New Deal. Bennett stated at that time: "I am for reform. And in my mind, reform means government intervention. It means government control and regulation. It means the end of laissez-faire."[1] He implemented a new legislative program that prepared the ground for Canada's universal social programs and social safety net. Under the Liberal prime ministers who followed him, William Lyon Mackenzie King and Louis St. Laurent, over the first few postwar decades, social programs were expanded, income was redistributed through higher taxes, and inequality began to decline. Health care and other social programs were brought under the public umbrella.

The tides did not begin to turn on this agenda until the 1980s, which ushered in a new era of tax cuts, social program cuts, and anti-government rhetoric. This new era was launched by U.S. President Ronald Reagan, British Prime Minister Margaret Thatcher, and, in Canada, Conservative Prime Minister Brian Mulroney, who was a product of the corporate elite. The pace of change has gained momentum since his tenure. Over the past three decades, taxes have been cut, social programs have been curtailed, inequality has been rising, poverty has been growing, and wealth has been increasingly concentrated at the top. The culmination has been the rise to federal power of the right-of-centre Conservative Party and the ascendancy of that party's radical right wing, which its poster boy, Prime Minister Stephen Harper, has lifted to a majority government in Ottawa.

What Led to This Turning of the Tides?

This dramatic change in economic and social policy has been no coincidence. But Brian Mulroney, Ronald Reagan, and Margaret Thatcher were not its instigators. Rather, this change was the direct result of a concerted campaign by corporations and the conservative movement to regain control of the policy agenda and the political landscape. That campaign began back in the early 1970s as a response to the New Deal postwar social and economic policy agenda.

Some powerful corporate interests viewed the postwar economic order as a serious threat. Specifically, that order was seen as an attack on the "enterprise system," "capitalism," and the "profit system." This was well summarized in the now-famous Powell Memo. In 1971, Lewis F. Powell, an American corporate lawyer and member of the boards of eleven corporations, wrote a memo to his friend Eugene Sydnor, Jr., Chairman of the Education Committee of the U.S. Chamber of Commerce, in which he stated: "No thoughtful person can question that the American economic system is under broad attack.... We are not dealing with sporadic or isolated attacks from a relatively few extremists or even from the minority socialist cadre. Rather, the assault on the enterprise system is broadly based and consistently pursued. It is gaining momentum and converts."[2]

Given the anti-communist culture of the Cold War era, it is not surprising that he mentions the Communists, New Leftists, and other revolutionaries. He notes, however, that they remain a small minority and that he does not see them as the principal cause for concern.

He does, however, raise the alarm about more mainstream voices: "The most disquieting voices joining the chorus of criticism come from perfectly respectable elements of society: from the college campus, the pulpit, the media, the intellectual and literary journals, the arts and sciences, and from politicians."[3] He specifically mentions university graduates who favour the public ownership of corporations.

Though they were hardly a national threat at the time he was writing, Powell in his memo names these social democrats as mortal enemies of the enterprise system and, by extension, of the economy as a whole.

The Powell Memo did more than raise the alarm for corporate interests: it issued a serious call to arms. Its author perceived the threat as one that required a co-ordinated response from a much better organized conservative movement. He recommended that the Chamber of Commerce organize a concerted fight-back on ground that extended far outside the boardrooms: "Survival of what we call the free enterprise system lies in organization, in careful long-range planning and implementation, in consistency of action over an indefinite period of years, in the scale of financing available only through joint effort, and in the political power available only through united action and national organizations." He outlined a clear program of action for taking back control of the economic agenda.

The Chamber of Commerce took up this challenge and helped mobilize a powerful conservative movement. And the American conservative movement was paralleled by a similar albeit smaller-scale co-ordinated effort in Canada. The Canadian movement has taken inspiration from the American one. Stephen Harper stated in a speech eight years ago to a conservative American think tank: "America, and particularly your conservative movement, is a light and an inspiration to people in this country and across the world."[4]

A clear policy platform for the aggressive protection and expansion of the enterprise system resulted from Powell's memo and has been consistently advocated by this co-ordinated movement.

Framing by the Right

Successful messaging has been a key element in the dramatic rise of the right-wing conservative movement.

The right wing's initiatives have been underpinned by an important concept often referred to as the Overton window, named after Joseph Overton, who developed it at the Mackinac Center, an American conservative think tank. The concept is based on a line representing the spectrum of policy options on a particular issue, from left to right. The Overton window represents the policy options that are currently feasible – that is, the options that are being discussed in current public debates and that a government can implement today without risking losing an election. The way to pull the window towards one side or the other is to start talking *outside* that window. Moving the window makes the unthinkable thinkable, and then doable, and then public policy.[5]

The window is based on the premise that new ideas, and the policy space to talk about them, are created outside government. It presumes that politicians, aware that they face re-election, will lean towards ideas within the window and that they are rarely ready to take a risk on an idea that is outside the window.

To move the window, it is necessary to discuss policy options that make people squirm; if the goal is to move that window, then the policy options and debates need to be outside it. The conservative movement brought the expansionist era of liberal social democracy to an end by being bold: by not being afraid to say things that were unpopular and by repeating them forcefully, and shamelessly. In this effort, the conservative movement has not been constrained by the facts or by what is politically palatable or even feasible. Indeed, the rhetoric of the right is increasingly being referred to as post-reality politics.[6]

A glaring example of this post-reality politics is Stephen Harper's statement: "I don't believe that any taxes are good taxes."[7] This is a patently irresponsible statement, coming as it does from the person elected to manage the nation's collective wealth; it is also obviously untrue. Given that he passes bills that increase military spending, he clearly supports taxation for such causes. Also, taken to its logical conclusion, no taxes at all would lead to no government, no infrastructure, and complete anarchy, which obviously would not be in the interests of the corporate elite he serves.

Grover Norquist is another excellent example of the conservative movement's post-reality vision and values. He is a right-wing lobbyist and a well-known organizer, activist, and spokesperson for the American far-right conservative movement. He is the author of a book titled *Leave Us Alone: Getting the Government's Hands Off Our Money, Our Guns, Our Lives.*

Ironically, the wealthy elites demand far more government intervention than any other interest group – witness the bailouts for the "too big to fail" banks during the 2008 financial crisis. Notwithstanding its anti-government and anti-spending rhetoric, the conservative movement has supported government intervention and spending. And this applies not just to those absurd bailouts, but to security as well. As inequality rises, so too does violence and unrest. Thus, in addition to corporate welfare, the movement supports significant increases in spending on police, prisons, and the military. These patterns can be seen clearly in Stephen Harper's budgets, which run directly counter to his rhetoric.

The rhetoric of this post-reality politics is patently absurd as an economic policy agenda. But it is not about policy; rather, it is about mobilizing support through value-laden rhetoric that generates suspicion of government and the public sector. This post-reality rhetoric helps build support for attacks on the public sector, as well as for cuts to taxes and the programs those taxes pay for.

Profits and Politics

The conservative movement's strength has been its clear and co-ordinated vision, the goals of which are to protect and increase corporate profits and expand the "free market." Norquist famously articulated that goal: "I'm not in favor of abolishing the government. I just want to shrink it down to the size where we can drown it in the bathtub." In the debates within that movement as to how to reduce the size of government, another quote sums it up well: "Starve the beast" – the beast, of course, being government, and the way to starve it being to cut taxes. Thus has emerged the mantra for tax cuts and social program cuts, which have been the goals of the conservative movement for decades.

A Compelling Narrative

The Overton window suggests that the key to changing government policy is to change public opinion. Another important element of the Overton window is that doing so takes more than facts and logic. Joseph G. Lehman, the President of the Mackinac Center, cautions that winning the battle for people's hearts and minds through economic analysis alone is "like bringing a knife to a gun fight." He contends that moral and emotional arguments are critical to moving the window to the right along the spectrum.

The right has developed a compelling story that has captured the imaginations and hearts of the public: that the wealthy and corporations are the only ones responsible enough to invest wisely and create jobs and thus should be the ones with the wealth; that the poor are poor because they are unworthy; that those who work hard get rewarded by becoming wealthy and successful; and that those who remain poor are irresponsible and make poor choices and thus should not be given money. The basic right-wing premise is that corporations and the wealthy will invest in ways that benefit all – that those investments will create jobs, opportunities, and more wealth for all, wealth that will trickle down to those at the bottom. This myth has been repeated often enough that many now take it as a fact, especially in the mainstream media. It has been repeated so often and so loudly that raising taxes has become synonymous with cutting jobs.

Yet the facts directly contradict the narrative. As will be shown later in this chapter, corporations are rewarded financially for *cutting* jobs; wealth does not trickle down but is being concentrated increasingly at the top; increased profits are too rarely translating into job growth; and many of the poor are locked into poverty *by* their poverty. But the right wing has crafted its own narrative so compellingly and repeated it so often that it is now more powerful than the facts.

The narrative of the right does not reflect any actual belief that a rising tide will raise all ships, or that the wealthy will use their largesse for the good of all; it is simply a cover for an economic and political project to increase the power and profits for the few. It reflects an agenda that will allow the rich to get richer and corporations to gain more profit and control. It has been hugely successful on both fronts.

Driving the Wedge Between the Middle Class and the Poor

The conservative movement is calling for tax cuts that will disproportionately benefit the wealthy and corporations, so this approach has not been immediately popular with the broader public. When the right launched its initiative in the 1970s, tax cuts were outside the Overton window. Memories of the Great Depression were still so strong that most Canadians, even though they were enjoying economic prosperity, continued to feel vulnerable. Middle-income Canadians would walk by someone who was homeless and think, "There but for the grace of God go I." Remembering their own vulnerability, Canadians empathized with the less fortunate. This common cause, and a broader sense of fairness, were the basis of Canadians' broad support for universal social programs.

To demonize government and undermine social programs, the conservative movement needed to drive a wedge between middle-income earners and the poor. It needed middle-income earners to identify more with the wealthy than with the less fortunate. So it undertook a concerted campaign to demonize the poor and characterize them as the sole authors of their fate.

That campaign has been remarkably successful – so much so that the window has shifted. The homeless and the poor have come to be seen as "other." The poor are being feared more and more by the broader public and blamed for their own plight in the media. This is evident in policies against panhandling and in the increasing criminalization of the poor. It is also evident in the stratification of poverty. In recent decades, social assistance has been gutted across Canada and social programs have been reshaped to reflect different classes of poor – the "deserving" (those with disabilities) and the undeserving (those deemed able to work). Higher incomes and more comprehensive benefits are given to the "deserving" poor.

The right wing's initiative has succeeded so well at shifting the Overton window that the NDP in B.C. gutted welfare as much as or more than the Conservatives did in Ontario in the 1990s.

Middle-income Canadians now identify with the wealthy rather than the poor, even though most middle-income families are much closer to being dead poor and on the streets than they are to being rich. The myth of the meritocracy – that hard work is rewarded with riches – has been used as cover for the massive redistribution of wealth from the lower and middle classes to the wealthy.

The right wing's success at driving this wedge between the poor and the middle class has enabled it to fully implement its agenda. Corporate excesses and luxuries enjoyed by the wealthy are not recognized as unfair; indeed, they are proffered as realistic goals for the middle class.

Progressives and the Overton Window

The progressive movement is very uncomfortable talking about and tackling ideas that fall outside of the Overton window. Progressive parties often tend away from taking an "outlier position" on particular policy issues. A clear example is Alberta's royalty reform debate. The Alberta government appointed a hand-picked royalty panel to assess Alberta's royalty structure (royalties are the revenues the government gets from natural resources taken out of the ground by private companies) and whether or not the public was getting a fair share. The panel released a set of royalty reform recommendations, which the panel itself said was a compromise between public and corporate interests. The industry immediately began crying foul, while the environmental movement and the opposition parties backed the panel. With corporate interests crying foul and the public lining up behind the panel, it did not look like a compromise had been made. The government immediately began backroom meetings with industry and threw out its own panel's report, seriously compromising the public interest.

Yet the panel was only calling for Alberta to move from the absolute bottom to somewhere in the basement for royalties internationally. More than three-quarters of the world's oil is nationally owned. This means that the private, for-profit international oil companies (IOCs) can't get access to it or can only access it under stringent conditions. Placing Alberta's royalty rates closer to the top in terms of international comparisons is hardly a revolutionary concept. Yet in backroom conversations, one opposition party stated, "We will not be an outlier on this."

Opposition parties on the centre-left are afraid to be portrayed as radical, and many not-for-profit and environmental organizations (except for

Greenpeace and perhaps a few others) rely on donors that may not appreciate initiatives that speak outside the window. Meanwhile, unions have their own constituencies to represent, which can make it a challenge for them to speak outside the window on some issues. Think tanks provide some counterbalance and indeed are often important players.

In the royalty reform example, the University of Alberta think tank, the Parkland Institute, stepped into the breach and published a report that was critical of the panel's recommendations and outside the window. It was profiled heavily in the mainstream media, and this in turn opened up policy space for opposition parties and NGOs to be more critical.

It is time for progressives to become much bolder in their policy conversations. It is time for the movement to recruit alternative voices that together will finds ways to move the window back towards the left. It is time, put more simply, to mobilize the resources for more co-ordinated action.

The Machinery

It is not enough to have the right messages; we also need the machinery to engage target groups and broader society with those messages. The strategy needs to be more comprehensive. According to sociologists at the American-based Media Research and Action Project, "to counter the assumption that the frame will set us free, framing strategies must not just address the content of the message or the style of debate but attend to base building and challenge the contours of the non-level playing field in which the contest is carried on."[8]

The Powell Memo laid out, for the right, a clear set of strategies for building a movement and for gaining control of key nodes for influencing both public opinion and government. First, it called for co-ordinated action, with corporations engaging in a long-range project through the network of Chambers of Commerce. The memo then targeted key vehicles of social and political influence, starting with universities. It called for the movement to build a staff of scholars and of speakers, to evaluate textbooks and demand equal time on campuses. Then it went even further, advocating for a "balancing of faculties" and for careful efforts to get corporate-friendly members of its movement onto university administrations and boards of trustees. It noted that this would be a difficult and long-term project. The Powell Memo also recommended that the movement gain access to and control over the media, resort to the courts, and involve itself heavily in politics with the goal of gaining political power.

The conservative movement diligently and efficiently built the infrastructure it needed. In "Tentacles of Rage" (2004), *Harper's Magazine* editor Lewis Lapham documented the billions of dollars that this well-co-ordinated conservative movement had spent on achieving its goals and the octopus-like re-education network that it had built.[9] He quoted the Chairman of the Democratic National Committee as saying this was "perhaps the most potent, independent institutionalized apparatus ever assembled in a democracy to promote one belief system."

In "Winner-Take-All Politics," renowned political scientists Jacob Hacker and Paul Pierson map out how the right has galvanized its resources and how corporate interests have set out to dominate the political system. They illustrate this with data such as the number of companies with registered lobbyists in Washington, which between 1971 and 1982 rose from 175 to nearly 2,500.[10]

In his summary, Lapham noted that Joseph Coors established The Heritage Foundation in 1973 with seed money of $250,000. That sum was augmented over the next few years with $900,000 from Richard Scaife. Then in the late 1970s, the American Enterprise Institute was revived and fortified with $6 million from the Howard Pew Freedom Trust. The Cato Institute was established by the Koch family in 1977 with a gift of $500,000. If in 1971 the friends of American free enterprise could turn for comfort to no more than seven not very competent sources of inspiration, by the end of the decade they could look to eight additional institutes committed to "joint effort" and "united action." The senior officers of the Fortune 500 companies meanwhile organized the Business Roundtable, providing it by 1979 with a rich endowment for hiring resident scholars who would be loyal in their opposition to taxes and anti-trust laws. They also went about acquiring media sources such as radio stations, newspapers, and journals, which would publicize the "research" that the think tanks' intellectual and propaganda machinery was to produce.

Those media outlets that were not outright owned were threatened with advertising strikes if they did not echo the social, political, and economic mantras of the right.

In 1979, Paul Weyrich of The Heritage Foundation and the Reverend Jerry Falwell formed the Moral Majority, which quickly became the organizing, lobbying, and activist arm of the religious right. This was a significant shift away from the prior alliance that many Christians had formed with the liberal left during the Great Depression.

In Canada, these trends have been paralleled to some extent, though moral and religious conservatism has been more successful in the United States, which has a different history and culture. Canada's first far-right propagandist think tank, the Fraser Institute, was founded in 1974 in Vancouver. It has since opened offices in Calgary, Toronto, Montreal, and Tampa, Florida. Other far-right think tanks that have merged religious and economic conservativism include the Manning Centre, the Institute for Marriage and the Family, and the Institute for Canadian Values.[11] Award-winning journalist Marci McDonald, in *The Armageddon Factor*, has carefully documented the multi-pronged integration of the conservative movement and the religious right in Canada and the many ties that both have developed with the Conservative government of Stephen Harper.[12] Add to these groups various narrowly economic conservative think tanks: the Frontier Centre for Public Policy, the Montreal Economic Institute, the Atlantic Institute for Market Studies, the C.D. Howe Institute, and the Macdonald–Laurier Institute.

The far right has a long history in Canada, with its nexus in Alberta, the Texas of the North. The Reform Party under Preston Manning and its successor, the Canadian Alliance, provided the far right with much of its ideology. More recently, Alberta has developed its own version of the Tea Party: the Wildrose Party under Fraser Institute–trained Danielle Smith. Smith is ramping up the heat under fiscal conservatism with its calls for tax cuts. Smith's key advisers and her political operatives are the same team that worked on Stephen Harper's election campaign, led by conservative strategist Tom Flanagan.

Labour and Citizens' Voices Denied

As the machinery of the right waxed, the power and influence of organized labour waned. The conservative movement launched a concerted attack on labour by generating and perpetuating the myth that unions stand in the way of efficiency, innovation, and job creation. The right-wing narrative demonized unions just as it had government and the public sector. This attack on labour rights has reversed the union movement's growth and shifted the balance of power among institutions. Having reached its peak of 38.6 per cent in 1982, the percentage of unionized Canadian workers had declined to 27.5 per cent by 2010, and most of the unionized workers who were left were in the public sector.

According to Hacker and Pierson, "the net effect of these diverse organizational shifts – the increasing organizational capacity of business, the decline of unions, the replacement of grassroots organizations with Washington-based managerial ones appealing to the affluent, the growing organizational clout of Christian conservatives, and the ever-increasing presence of big money in political life – is actually straightforward: they have dramatically weakened the *organized* political voice of ordinary citizens on economic issues."[13]

Power and Profit: A Recipe for Success?

The conservative movement has been remarkably successful; the "starve the beast" agenda is coming to fruition. The political mobilizing for tax cuts and social spending cuts has succeeded in serving the interests and maximizing the profits of the wealthy and their large corporations.

In Canada, the tax cut agenda has been implemented with almost unrivalled zeal. The federal corporate income tax rate stood at 28 per cent in 2000. This was cut to 21 per cent under the Liberals, and then cut in stages, from 21 to 15 per cent, under the Conservatives. The most recent cut was from 16.5 to 15 per cent, effective January 1, 2012. As of 2012, Canada has the dubious distinction of applying the lowest corporate tax rates in the G8.

The right-wing agenda really has hit pay dirt when it comes to corporate profits and private incomes. Corporate profits have begun a steady rise, with slight blips for the recession, reaching new records year over year. Canada's largest corporations are making 50 per cent more profit and paying 20 per cent less tax than they were a decade ago.[14] And what are they doing with all that money? They have been ramping up both dividend payouts and accumulations of assets. Dividends as a share of after-tax profits have risen from 30 per cent in 2000 to over 50 per cent in recent years. For every dollar in after-tax profit, 49 cents has gone to shareholders.[15]

This reality belies the conservative narrative of growth, job creation, and the trickling down of wealth. Statistics Canada reports that even while the economy has been growing, productive investment has stagnated. Real investment in buildings, machinery, and equipment has fallen as a share of the economy, in lockstep with corporate tax rates. The TD Bank reported before the recession that the ratio of business investment to profits had fallen to an all-time low.

Income concentration has followed a similar gold vein for those at the top. According to the Organization for Economic Co-operation and Development (OECD), Canada's rich have been getting richer and the poor poorer. Canada's richest 1 per cent took almost one-third (32 per cent) of all growth in incomes between 1997 to 2007.[16] The right-wing conservative agenda has led to trickle-*up* economics and made a lie of the mantra that a rising tide raises all ships.

Inequality has been skyrocketing in Canada. Among the 17 wealthiest developed countries, Canada now ranks 14th for inequality and poverty.

Towards a Progressive Narrative

The right-wing narrative has consistently shown itself to be false. The financial crisis and rising inequality have exposed the dark underbelly of the right's relentless drive for profit. Yet its narrative continues to prevail.

Raising awareness that the conservative narrative is false will require a great deal of work. Like the Mackinac Center says, "the facts are not enough." It is not enough to prove that the right-wing story in false. Until the progressive movement comes up with a compelling narrative that speaks to the values of the public, the Overton window will not move to the left.

Progressives have been very successful in Canada at moving the window on social policy issues but have had much less success on the economic side. Witness the meteoric rise and fall of the Wildrose Party, Alberta's equivalent to the Tea Party, in the last provincial election there. According to many of the polls, the party was heading for majority government territory. Then some of the party's candidates made socially conservative comments, such as that homosexuals would burn in a lake of eternal fire, and other comments that were clearly racist. The party stalled in its momentum and lost the election badly to the Conservatives. Both Stephen Harper and Wildrose's Danielle Smith have backed away from hard-core social conservative messages. Progressives have been very successful in their battle against social conservatism.

On economic issues, the left has been far less successful. The left needs to move beyond the facts and the moral arguments. It needs to develop a strong and co-ordinated movement to counter the right's powerful machinery.

High debt levels, punishing workloads, and stress combined with losses from the financial crisis and recession have left middle-class Canadians feeling more vulnerable than they have since the Great Depression. Meanwhile, the Occupy Movement has raised awareness about the concentration of wealth and the unfairness of economic booms and busts.

The moment is ripe for removing the wedge from between poor and middle-income Canadians and driving it between the middle-income and the wealthy. And for exposing the corruption, nepotism, and excesses of the corporate sector, for making governments transparent and accountable, and for moderating the excesses of the corporate sector in ways that will protect Canadians from market turmoil.

Strong economic arguments are emerging that inequality must be ended. Consensus is growing that inequality is bad for both the economy and the well-being of all Canadians. Even the International Monetary Fund, a mainstream institution, has concluded that "helping raise the smallest boats may help keep the tide rising for all craft, big and small."[17] Its study of sustainable economic growth found that the most significant factor was income distribution, which was even more closely correlated than political institutions, trade openness, exchange rate competitiveness, external debt, and foreign direct investment.

Richard Wilkinson and Kate Pickett have provided material to expand that narrative to quality of life for all – wealthy and poor alike.[18] Their data indicate that less equal societies are correlated with the following:

- Poorer physical health (shorter life expectancy, higher infant mortality, and reduced "self-rated" health).
- Poorer mental health (far more mental illness).
- Drug abuse (higher incidence of addiction, more likelihood of using illegal drugs).
- Poorer education outcomes.
- More imprisonment.
- Higher obesity rates.
- Less social mobility.
- Communities that are less cohesive, in which people trust one another less.
- Increased violent crime, including higher homicide rates and more violence against children.
- Higher teenage pregnancy rates.
- Poorer child well-being.

Finally, progressives can raise awareness that policy is being made in the interests of the wealthy and corporations at the expense of the middle class. Also, that the current electoral system is fundamentally anti-democratic and leaves many out in the cold. No elected government will change that system, for they benefit from it, but a progressive movement should root its narrative in real democracy in which every vote counts. An Environics poll commissioned by the Council of Canadians and carried out in February 2011 found that fully 62 per cent of Canadians support a change in the voting system to one using proportional representation.

A lesson that the left can learn from the right is that attack is the best defence. It is time for progressives to take the gloves off and call out the corporations for their excesses and the wealthy for taking more than their share and for damaging everyone's quality of life.

Progressives also need to recognize that a focus on party politics will not be enough. As long as the Overton window remains so far to the right, any elected party will find itself compelled to operate within it and drift right. A strong progressive movement is needed to move the Overton window. The left can learn from the right that it needs to expand its infrastructure in order to strengthen and unify itself; also, that it needs to develop a clear narrative capable of shifting the window for all political parties. Progressives need to galvanize more resources, with the focus on media, think tanks, university campuses, lobbying, and litigating. Most important, this effort needs to be focused on messages that are currently outside the Overton window – on bold and sometimes even uncomfortable ideas and policy options.

Progressives need to talk about tax increases, about social programs being expanded, about strengthening labour rights, and about *all* poor people (not just children or the disabled) deserving dignity and respect. Given the failure of the market economy and the corporations that dominate and profit from it to provide a reasonable and sustainable income for Canadians despite all the corporate coddling that goes on, why *not* take society's wealth and redistribute it with a social wage for all? Why *not* index taxes to target rates of inequality? Why *not* charge foreign oil companies a premium rather than a discount for access to Canada's strategic non-renewable resources? Why give them access at all when over 90 per cent of the rest of the world's oil is publicly owned? Only if the left talks aggressively and consistently about ideas far outside the current window – ideas such as public ownership, tax increases, and more universal social programs – will it be able to move the window.

The economist Paul Krugman has written: "Actually turning [the United States] around is going to take years of siege warfare against deeply entrenched interests, defending a deeply dysfunctional political system."[19] As Stephen Harper continues to Americanize Canada, Krugman's words ring increasingly true for our nation as well. Canada is less and less recognizable. Harper's government is dismantling our social programs, undermining universality, blackening our international reputation, expanding our military, building more prisons to incarcerate more of the poor and mentally ill, and implementing the conservative corporate agenda. Our political system is deeply dysfunctional. Turning it around will take co-ordinated effort by a strong and well-organized progressive movement.

3

The Power of Conventional Thinking

Canada's Media Join the Anti-Tax Movement

RICHARD SWIFT

JOURNALISM, WHATEVER ITS HIGHER-MINDED PRETENSIONS, is first and foremost a business. Press barons like Rupert Murdoch and Conrad Black are capitalists as rapacious as you will find anywhere. So it should surprise no one that newspaper publishers have usually sided with the rich and powerful in other industries. They allow space on their pages for a few discordant voices, but overall, they side with big business and make its preoccupations their own. That is why, when it comes to tax policy, the mainstream media very much reflect the anti-tax bias of the conservative movement and the business elite. A look at the structure of print journalism in Canada gives a sense of why this is so.

"Virtually all of Canada's 98 city newspapers as well as the two national dailies have special business sections that sometimes are larger than the paper's regular news sections," Nick Fillmore points out on Rabble.ca. "One small-city chain has a weekly page called 'Money.' At least half a dozen magazines are devoted entirely to business, and the country has hundreds of business trade publications. In addition, dozens of U.S. business publications flood across the border into Canada."[1]

In this chapter I will show how the business community influences mainstream journalism – that is, how it frames economic news coverage in ways that advance a consistently anti-tax message. In most of Canada's media, the issue of tax justice is missing in action. Right-wing neoliberalism is the order of the day, and it responds in knee-jerk fashion to any opposing views. The entire range of alternative economic thought from

Keynesianism moving left is severely underrepresented. In mainstream financial reporting, the coverage and commentary is overwhelmingly sympathetic to the anti-tax message, which is based on a number of sadly predictable notions:

- Governments waste large amounts of public funds.
- Sharp cutbacks in expenditures are needed to rein in out-of-control spending and to reduce deficits.
- Tax increases of any type are bad economics and suicidal politics.

A number of assumptions have shaped these views. One of these is the persistent bias, especially in the English-language media, that markets must be unfettered if economies are to grow.

This view has its roots in the economic theories of figures like F.A. Hayek and Paul Samuelson and its branches in the pro-business, neoliberal public policies that gained ascendancy among mainstream journalists in the 1980s. These were the years of Margaret Thatcher, Ronald Reagan, and Brian Mulroney, when conservative and libertarian theorists argued that free markets are "natural" and that societies tamper with them at their own peril. This view of markets, though, denies the simple and indeed fundamental fact that market arrangements are created by human beings, a small cohort of whom have always used governments to enact and enforce their own rules for them. Without contract laws and laws to protect property, orderly markets would be impossible. During the years of rampant speculation in the 1990s and early 2000s, investment gurus talked enthusiastically about "market making" and concocted dangerous new financial instruments to "securitize" everything from weather predictions to bundled sub-prime mortgages.

In the mainstream news coverage of business, the all-too-human origins of markets have been forgotten. In that coverage, the *real* markets, with their human winners and losers, have been replaced with a fantasy market – an economic state of nature – that supposedly, when left to its own devices, runs with near-perfect equilibrium as it allocates risks and resources. This view is, of course, especially appealing to market winners, who don't want governments to tamper with arrangements that benefit them. The notion that there is a "natural" market is reinforced by popular nostrums that appeal to the economically illiterate and that underpin much of the coverage provided by journalists who should know better – nostrums like "a rising tide raises all boats" and "wealth created at the top trickles down to benefit the rest of us." Ideas about business confidence and the primacy of the private over the public have become mantras in the business sections of today's newspapers.

Tax Freedom Day

The most controversial economic issue of all is taxation. This is where the rubber hits the road – where private stops and public begins. Taxation is too often portrayed as a subtraction from human well-being that disappears into the ether of government waste and debt. Echoing tales about feudal lords seizing tribute of grain and pigs from hard-working peasants, many journalists champion the poor benighted taxpayer as a victim of the rapacious state. That view, which now permeates economic and business coverage, has crystallized perhaps most clearly in the notion of Tax Freedom Day.

Tax Freedom Day was founded in 1948 by a Florida businessman named Dallas Hostetler as a way of measuring the amount of time in a year one "works" for the government before finally breaking free and being allowed to work for oneself. The idea is misleadingly simple: each dollar officially considered annual income by the government is added up; then all taxes and fees paid to all levels of government are subtracted from gross personal income. This is a way of calculating the number of days you (as a fictitious average person) work from the beginning of the year in order to pay the sum of the taxes and fees you will owe to various levels of government for the entire year. The day this tax burden is totally funded is then declared Tax Freedom Day. That day has become the stick that anti-tax fiscal conservatives use to beat their drum. It is calculated by right-wing advocacy groups such as the Washington-based Tax Foundation and the Vancouver-based Fraser Institute. Free market advocates and think tanks in some twenty-five countries use Tax Freedom Day to advance their cause – though the days are not strictly comparable because of variations in the calculations used. In 2010, Tax Freedom Day in the United States was calculated as falling on April 9; in Canada, it didn't roll around until May 2.[2] A year earlier, Canadians had been "slaves" of the state until June 6. Sober-minded assessments of Tax Freedom Day suggest that it is simply a tool for measuring how long we have to work in order to pay for public services. However, there is very little about Tax Freedom Day that is sober-minded. More often, that day is the occasion for an unrestrained assault on wasteful government expenditures – one that largely ignores the social goods delivered through public expenditures, which include education, health care, public order, social safety nets for unemployed, poor, sick, and old people, and a range of publicly supported cultural activities. Citizens are encouraged to think of themselves solely as self-interested taxpayers and to ask themselves whether they are getting value for money. Citizenship and the health of society are sacrificed on the altar of "get your hands out of my pockets." With a few exceptions, the media pick up the beat and amplify the Tax Freedom Day message out into the public.

Thoughtful journalists could instead propose a Mortgage Freedom Day or a Price Freedom Day, when one stops paying banks and corporations the excessive amounts that allow CEOs to draw multimillion-dollar salaries and bonuses. However, such things are in the private realm and are determined by the magic of the free market, which is not to be questioned and with which there can be no tampering. The Canadian Taxpayers Federation has its own approach to promoting an anti-tax perspective through the media: every year for the past twelve, it has given out the Teddy Awards to highlight what it considers particularly egregious examples of government waste. There are as yet no awards handed out to those who expose tax avoidance by Canada's well-to-do. The programs that the CTF considers worth exposing as waste suggest the political biases of the anti-tax movement: "gold-plated pensions" for politicians rank high, and so do "wasteful" social surveys of Toronto's homeless population, but the building of expensive new mega-prisons and the dispatching of Canadian soldiers to fight in distant wars do not. Left-leaning politicians are especially likely targets: former Toronto mayor David Miller got a lifetime achievement award in 2011 for his spending habits.[3]

There have been very few systematic studies of how the Canadian media cover tax policy. The ones that *have* been conducted show a clear anti-tax populist bias, one that promotes the assumption that the

Canadian tax system is wasteful and overcomplicated and is dragging the country down. One such study is Larry Patriquin's *Inventing Tax Rage* (2004), which examines how the *National Post* systematically exaggerates (and at times invents) the damage that mildly progressive taxation is supposedly doing to the Canadian economy. Patriquin describes how the *Post* plays with issues such as the supposed "complexity" of the tax system in order to advocate changes that would largely benefit the upper tiers of Canadian taxpayers. He credits the *Post*'s campaign with helping bring about a massive shift in the tax system. "In its first three years of operation," he writes, "the *Post* reportedly lost $200 million. However, this was a shrewd investment, compared to a return of roughly $150 billion in federal tax cuts over the period 1997–2005. The *National Post* was a stroke of brilliance on the part of the Canadian Right, an act of hubris perhaps unequaled in the Western world over the past few decades."[4]

This may go some way to explaining what has puzzled many observers: why a national daily that has always lost money has managed to avoid being closed by otherwise fairly savvy owners. Patriquin lays out a series of strategies that *Post* journalists and columnists have used to foster the public mood for tax cuts. Those strategies include portraying the top 1 per cent who benefit from tax cuts as part of the "middle class," and exaggerating the benefits of the cuts to most Canadians while hiding their costs: declining social services, as well as user fees that, for most people, swamp whatever minor tax cuts they receive. The *Post* is perhaps an extreme example of this sleight of hand, and most other media are perhaps fairer in their coverage. But the *Post* has done much to set the tone for journalists at other outlets, such as the *Globe and Mail*'s *Report on Business*, who sing from the same songbook most of the time. It is also worth noting that the *Post* is the flagship paper in a chain of national newspapers and other media outlets (CanWest Global Communications) and sets the editorial tone for the rest.

Quantitative studies are of limited use in media criticism but do indicate the preoccupations built into media agendas. In a 2009 issue of *International Tax Notes*, in a case study titled "How Canada's Flat Tax Debate Played in the Press," Thaddeus Hwong combines quantitative analysis with a close reading of the Canadian media. His subject is the media coverage of a campaign run by the conservative Fraser Institute in favour of a simplified flat tax to replace the progressive income tax. The flat tax has long been proposed by the anti-tax Right. Under the banner of tax simplification, the flat tax would squeeze revenues to downsize government while shifting tax obligations away from the wealthiest. In 2008 the Fraser Institute released a study it titled *The Impact and Cost of Taxation in Canada: The Case for Flat Tax Reform.* Hwong found the press highly receptive to the institute's initiative: "flat tax" generated 13,500 hits on the Internet between 2004 and 2009 while "income inequality" generated fewer than 9,000.[5] Hwong found that most of the press coverage the report generated – and there was a great deal of it – more or less recycled the controversial views of the Fraser Institute's press releases. That same coverage neglected to raise serious questions about some of the report's more questionable assertions, such as the notion that complying with the present tax system cost the Canadian economy between $19 and $31 billion a year in time, accountancy services, computer software, and so on. Most stories eagerly picked up on the idea that with a flat tax, Canadians would need only fill out a post-card every year (a few minutes' work) and send it to Revenue Canada. Those same stories gave short shrift to the main criticism of the flat tax – that it would shift the tax burden from the wealthy onto lower-income payers. And they failed to expose the obvious fact that far from being "revenue neutral," the flat tax was part of a strategy by economic conservatives to downsize government – including what most Canadians count on governments to provide – by "starving the beast" of sufficient revenue. Hwong's conclusion: Canada's media had starved the minds of Canadians of the critical intelligence they needed for an honest and open debate about taxation's impact on good governance.

Personal Finance Journalism

All of this has been reinforced by the rise of personal finance journalism. This branch of business reporting has become a media staple since the 1980s and takes up an increasing number of column inches in the business sections of the daily papers. In 2003, in a seminal magazine piece in *Harper's Magazine*, Bill Wasik described the evolution of this form of "how to" journalism:

Its purview should not be termed "business journalism," for other than the reader's profit motive, our business periodicals disregard nearly every aspect of business and its effect on our lives. Instead, one might call it "personal-finance journalism": its reporting provides a resource for the reader to consult in his portfolio management, her career counseling. In other subject areas, such writing is sequestered under the rubric of "service journalism," but personal finance journalism is the dominant mode of business writing in America today, if not the only mode. From its grip the business press shows few signs of emerging.[6]

This form of advice journalism has arrived north of the border and taken a firm grip on Canadian economic journalism. The idea is to appeal to an "investor society" by reaching for readers who do not inhabit or have a direct stake in the financial industry. It would be a mistake, though, to lionize the financial and economic coverage of the past. In earlier times, much space was devoted to the personalities and philosophies of the corporate elite and to gossip about who was rising and who was falling. The journalism of that doyen of Canadian business journalism, Peter C. Newman, largely took that form.

There has always been muckraking journalism, which sometimes exposes the underbelly of big business. This tradition continues today, albeit in a muted fashion, in the *Toronto Star* (especially in its coverage of the Canadian mining industry), at the CBC, and occasionally elsewhere. Yet even the CBC, which thoughtful Canadians have turned to for generations, is showing signs of capitulating to the ethic of market *über alles*. Take the example of market libertarian Michael Hlinka, who provides daily radio commentary on CBC's *Metro Morning* in Toronto. That radio slot has recently been adjusted; Armine Yalnizyan of the Centre for Policy Alternatives has begun to sit in for Hlinka twice a week. Perhaps the CBC got tired of bending over backwards to accommodate the conservative Right, for which it was rewarded with a further 10 per cent cut to its budget. Right-of-centre commentary from people like pundit Rex Murphy and *Maclean's* market libertarian Andrew Coyne still dominates editorializing on CBC TV. *Maclean's* itself, once a weekly touchstone for the Canadian middle class, has become a kind of right-wing pamphlet that makes *Time* and *Newsweek* look balanced.

Today, financial journalism on the whole is much more closely integrated with business and investor concerns. The focus on personal finance journalism is just a part of this. The flavour of this form of journalism is evident in *Report on Business*, the *Globe and Mail's* business magazine. Its advertising kit proudly declares its target audience: "written by experts ... for the people in power at Canada's top corporations. It's pro-business, pro-Canada, pro-reader."[7] A certain amount of hyperbole should be allowed, to take into account the *ROB*'s desire (shared by the *Financial Post*, *Canadian Business* magazine, and others) to attract advertising from corporations by presenting itself as a hospitable environment for corporate concerns. In other words, it is not in these pages that one can expect campaigns – or even much coverage of campaigns – to increase corporate or any other kinds of taxes.

But defining your audience as "the people in power in Canada's top corporations" is obviously too limiting. For a start, that is far too small an audience to sustain a regular publication. It also prevents the *ROB* from spreading its corporate message more broadly. This is where personal finance journalism comes in. Over the past three decades, economic coverage has shifted; more space and air time is now being allotted to stories and opinion pieces that address the reader as a small investor, as a consumer of financial and other corporate products, and – what most concerns us here – as a taxpayer. This form of journalism provides advice on what kind of mortgage to take out, the best low-tax jurisdictions to retire to or keep your money in, which sectors or mutual fund products to invest in, and how best to reduce one's overall personal tax "burden." In concert with the initiatives surrounding Tax Freedom Day, this encourages readers to think of themselves as individual taxpayers trying to get as much as possible in services while paying as little as possible in taxes. While not encouraging tax evasion, which is illegal, it scours the tax code looking for loopholes and exemptions that readers might utilize to reduce their personal tax. This is tax avoidance (which is legal), rather than tax evasion (which is not). While people's desire to pay less tax is understandable enough, an anti-tax world view is implicit in this approach, which promotes and shapes "taxpayer thinking" as the alternative to any overall notion of citizenship that might value taxes and the public expenditures that taxes support. In this way, individual well-being replaces overall social health. So it is hardly a surprise that proposals to raise taxes – particularly on forms of investment income or through inheritance or corporate taxation – get a less than favourable reception in the media as a whole and in the financial pages in particular.

The Missing Issues

Much of the anti-tax message in the mainstream media reflects more absence than advocacy. The journalist Nick Fillmore encountered a clear example of this in his 2010 investigative piece on pro-business bias in the *Globe and Mail*. Fillmore focused on a *Globe* story about the privatization of Crown corporations in Ontario.[8] The provincial government, facing a deficit of $24.7 billion and growing, was considering selling off (or whole or in part) institutions like Hydro One and the Alcohol and Gaming Commission of Ontario – both are major contributors to the province's public coffers. In December 2009, the *Globe* floated a speculative front-page story by two *Report on Business* journalists under the headline "Ontario Looks to Unload Crown Corporations." Fillmore found this story (and its follow-ups) unbalanced, speculative, and misleading. Some of its sources were described as "unnamed investment bankers." The sales would have been hugely controversial, softened only by the emotive resort to deficit reduction – a concept utilized by much of the political class and the conservative press as cover for their anti-tax, anti-spending agenda. Missing from this and from much other coverage of deficit economics was any serious discussion of tax increases on corporations and the wealthy as an alternative deficit-fighting strategy.

The media barely cover let alone debate many serious tax issues, such as whether the personal income tax rate for upper-income Canadians should be increased, whether capital gains taxes should remain as low as they are, and whether the corporate tax rate should be raised instead of cut. Canada is the only Western country without some form of inheritance tax, but this fact remains virtually unknown to most Canadians and is largely absent from media discussion. The country is facing severe problems in public finance, so a debate about tax justice and the inequalities built into the current tax system would seem sensible. But the silence has been deafening.

The tax cutters have this advantage: the tax code is more regressive today than at any time since the Second World War. Yet they continue to rail against taxes as a drag on the economy. Listen to the language that Andrew Coyne uses to describe the McGuinty government in a *Maclean's* article in support of harmonizing the federal and provincial sales taxes. Spending is "careening" out of control. The province is "perilously close to a fiscal precipice."[9] Coyne sometimes sounds as if Ontario is approaching the fate of bankrupt Greece: "[McGuinty] has raised taxes (when he promised he wouldn't), ramped up spending at an alarming rate, and repealed rather than obey[ed] the province's balanced budget law. He has handed out hundreds of millions of dollars to failing automakers, picked pointless fights with the feds, and overseen the province's decline into have-not status."

Yet despite this supposed tax profligacy, McGuinty's government (which cut corporate taxes) has failed to provide poor Ontarians with welfare rates they can live on and has actually cut the dietary Special Needs Allowance for the needy. In the Ontario 2011 election, McGuinty was portrayed as "the taxman" by his Conservative opponents as if they were going to halt taxation entirely if they gained power.

Canada has become so tax-friendly for the rich that they are coming here from all over the world under the auspices of Canada's Immigration Investor Program. In 2010 almost 12,000 people took advantage of this program, which is open only to those with assets of at least $1.6 million. Long waiting lists of the wealthy seeking to settle (or at least buy a luxury condo) in Canada have Immigration Minister Jason Kenney drooling as he talks about new programs for fast-tracking high-income immigrants, especially "high-value innovators." The *Globe's ROB* has reported enthusiastically on new initiatives to attract the wealthy but has made no mention of the draconian restrictions being introduced for those seeking political asylum.[10] Referring to Canada's lax taxation laws, Tom McCullough, CEO of Northwood Family Office, has called Canada "the Switzerland of North America." Northwood is a boutique Toronto firm that advises families with assets of between $10 million and $500 million. McCullough is keen to spread the message that "Canada offers a surprisingly-attractive tax regime for high net worth immigrants, while housing a world-class professional services and financial infrastructure."[11]

The wealthy, whether prospective immigrants or already Canadian, are clearly happy with the lack of inheritance tax, the declining rate of corporate taxation, and Finance Minister Jim Flaherty's commitment to further flatten the tax system (he plans to reduce the number of tax brackets once the budget deficit is under control). They also appreciate, one would assume, that tax injustice is not an issue in most of Canada's media.

The Missing Opinions

The leftists in Canadian politics claim that there is a pervasive media bias against them. The rightists claim the same thing. Yet if you web-search "media bias Canada," the large majority of complaints that pop up at the top of the listings are from conservative organizations or from bloggers such as the Frum Forum. For them, mild centrism on social issues is left-wing extremism. Their most recent cause has been the championing of Sun TV, a kind of Fox News right-wing clone for Canada. Despite lobbying from the Harper government, the CRTC has so far denied the Quebecor-owned station preferential status on the TV dial. So far the station has been characterized by non-stop right-wing editorializing posing as news, with host Ezra Levant, who seems to be on camera 24/7, doing most of the ranting.

There is a growing body of right-wing opinion in Canada that the current Conservative government has sold its values out. Terence Corcoran, editor of the *Financial Post* as well as one of its columnists, and a hardcore libertarian, used his pulpit after the 2011 federal Conservative victory to bemoan the centrist nature of the Harper government.[12] Andrew Coyne had set the tone back in 2009 with a *National Post* piece whining about the Conservatives' lack of rigour in imposing tax cuts and privatizations.[13] Significant voices in the Canadian media have positioned themselves well to the right of Harper's Conservatives. Meanwhile, it is hard to imagine those to the left of the NDP in Canada finding the resources, or the clout, to launch their own TV station (à la Sun TV) or newspaper chain (the Sun papers), or that they could land editorial posts in the present day's national print media (which include the *National Post*, *Maclean's*, and the *Globe and Mail*).

Perhaps the complaint about left-wing bias in the media (assuming it is not simply a pity-poor-us-swimming-against-the-current tactic) is rooted in the fact that most Canadian journalists are not social conservatives (in favour of banning abortion and imprisoning those guilty of "unreported crime," whatever that is) and remain skeptical of the motives of people in authority. Uncovering a story and revealing the seamy underside of power is part of the fun of a journalist's job. Stout patriotism and respect for traditional leadership are right-wing values that can get trampled in this media scrum. A lot of this belief in leftist media bias comes from across the border. As one American critic put it:

> The greatest con job ever pulled by the American right was the notion that the mainstream media (MSM) is overwhelmingly liberal. This false premise has not only permitted the creation of overtly partisan conservative media but it has caused the MSM to overbalance for fear of being perceived as liberal. The joke during George W. Bush's years in office was that if he announced the Earth was flat the headline would read "Shape of Planet in Dispute."[14]

In Canada much of this paranoia has attached itself to the beleaguered CBC, which has responded by bending over backwards to perceived conservative pressure.

However, when it comes to coverage of economic affairs in general and to taxing and spending issues in particular, the financial pages and most business reporters show a powerful bias in favour of neoliberal assumptions. Some of this is ideologically inspired. Some of it has to do with the individualistic standpoint adopted by personal finance journalism. But a great deal of it is because of shallow and lazy thinking. Journalists habitually quote "certified" spokespeople without question – bank economists, investment specialists from the brokerage industry, real estate executives, and spokespeople from major accounting or credit rating firms. These spokespeople are deployed as "experts" to tie up the story, and seldom are their (mostly neoliberal) values questioned. With the exception of the odd maverick, the drumbeat of opinion is depressingly conventional. Think tanks and other policy groups, most of them either conventional or ardently conservative in their economic thinking, are similarly utilized. These include the Conference Board of Canada, the C.D. Howe Institute, the Fraser Institute, the Canadian

Taxpayers Federation, the Rotman Business School, the Insurance Bureau of Canada, and the Canadian Federation of Independent Business, to name just a few. There are, of course, left-wing alternatives that get the occasional look-in – the Centre for Policy Alternatives, independent economists, perhaps a staffer at a trade union or an advocate for the poor. But because leftist groups are fewer in number and lack the resources they need to raise a high profile, alternative voices remain few and far between. The Hwong study, quoted above, quantified this bias:

> A search in Factiva for "Conference Board of Canada" generated 6,078 hits in the five-year period of 2004 through 2008, while a search for "Fraser Institute" generated 5,225 hits for the same period. C.D. Howe Institute, another conservative think tank in Canada, generated 2,976 hits over the five years. In contrast, a search for the progressive "Canadian Centre for Policy Alternatives" generated only 1,419 hits for the five years, while a search for "Caledon Institute of Social Policy" generated merely 117 hits.[15]

Some media make more of an effort to balance their stories (CBC Radio and the *Toronto Star*); others make hardly any at all.

Since the 1970s, the Canadian media have been criticized for wearing economic blinkers and for their lack of diversity. In the recent past, the Davey Commission (1970), the Kent Commission (1981), and most recently a Senate committee investigation (June 2006) have all pointed out these worrisome shortcomings. Nothing substantial has been or likely will be done about this, given the current political alignment. The status quo will mean that the right-wing, anti-tax, anti–public-sector biases will remain in place. The companies that control Canada's private media – Canwest Global, Rogers, Shaw, Quebecor, CTV Global Media, and Astral Media – are all very hospitable to this perspective. One need look no further than the fact that of the eighteen major newspapers in Canada, seventeen supported Steven Harper's Conservatives in his 2011 election victory (the exception being the *Toronto Star*). They can be counted on to hold his feet to the fire in the unlikely event that he falters in his tax-cutting commitments – "Oink! Another trip to the trough" is the level of commentary that can be expected of the *Toronto Sun*. All of this is helping maintain fiscal inequality while disguising tax cuts as a great advance in individual opportunity. As a recent example, the *Globe and Mail* (Canada's "paper of record") went into a hissy fit over the token 2 per cent surtax that the NDP forced on the Liberals as the price of support for their 2012 minority budget in the Ontario Legislature. The *Globe* fulminated that this grievous measure was "punishing success" and went on to opine that it was a slap to those who create jobs and wealth. Yet Ontario's highest tax rate (46 per cent) is at the lowest level since the Great Depression. The *Globe* remains silent on Ontario social assistance rates that buy 60 per cent less than they did in 1995. As Joe Hill demanded to know: "Which side are you on?"

The financial meltdown of 2008, which was followed directly by the sovereign debt crisis, has resulted in enforced austerity throughout the advanced economic world. Everywhere, fiscal conservatives have used those events as an excuse to do what they have always wanted to do – attack government social provisions for the less well-off, curtail the regulation of corporate misbehaviour, and launch an assault on the jobs and rights of public service workers. The federal Conservatives' spring 2012 budget followed suit – it rolled back pension rights, laid off federal workers, and cut a number of programs that made food safe, prisons more humane, and public broadcasting healthy. Around this time, Canadians for Tax Fairness held a national conference in Ottawa to look at the equity or lack of it on the revenue side of the public ledger. A number of well-known experts on tax policy gave presentations. Coverage by the Canadian media – even the usually sympathetic media – was non-existent. One ledger where the deficit certainly needs rebalancing is in media coverage obsessed with "wasteful" spending and blind to Canada's inadequate and unfair tax system.

4

The Trouble with Tax Havens

Whose Shelter? Whose Storm?

PETER GILLESPIE

TAX HAVENS ARE THE CENTREPIECES of a shadow financial system that enables users to escape tax laws and regulations in their own countries. Tax havens typically offer minimal regulation; little or no taxation on the income or capital of non-residents; legally enforced secrecy; non-disclosure of beneficial ownership of offshore corporations, trusts, and foundations; and no effective exchange of information with other countries. As John Christensen notes, these characteristics make such jurisdictions susceptible to a wide range of criminal and corrupt practices.[1] Yet they remain ubiquitous, protected, and immune from regulation and oversight.

What possible logic allows such a state of affairs to prevail?

In March 2011, Canada's Parliamentary Standing Committee on Finance held hearings on offshore bank accounts and tax evasion. Among the expert witnesses called to testify was a professor from the Rotman School of Management at the University of Toronto. In his remarks, the professor told parliamentarians that there are many positive benefits when Canadian companies make use of offshore financial centres. Canadian corporations become more competitive, he said, because of the lower taxes they pay when repatriating profits to Canada. Offshore centres are conduits for Canadian businesses to gain access to the global economy, allowing them entry to riskier markets and to emerging ones. While making it clear that he didn't endorse tax evasion, he said that because of the reduced cost of capital for Canadian companies, offshore centres are good for the Canadian economy.[2]

The professor's apologia for and endorsement of offshore tax havens

– more properly called secrecy jurisdictions – is astonishing given the economic damage they have inflicted on countries of both the North (including Canada) and the South. Multinational corporations and banking and financial institutions routinely use secrecy jurisdictions to lower or eliminate their tax obligations, avoid regulation, and obscure their financial transactions. Wealthy individuals hold trillions of dollars in offshore accounts, thereby avoiding the payment of taxes in their places of residence. Resources from some of the world's poorest countries have disappeared into offshore black holes, depriving them of the means to invest in schools, health services, and essential public infrastructure. Every year, more than US$1.5 trillion of criminal money – from drug smuggling, arms and human trafficking, and corruption – is laundered through secrecy jurisdictions.[3] All of these problems are linked to an opaque and unaccountable offshore system that festers at the heart of global finance.

The origin of offshore money laundering is linked to a rather disreputable period in Canadian history. The Prohibition era in the United States between 1919 and 1933 was a bonanza for American gangsters as well as for Canadian bootleggers such as Samuel Bronfman. Throughout the 1920s, millions of gallons of Canadian rye whiskey were smuggled across the border to a thirsty American populace. The American gangsters involved were a who's who of the underworld – Frank Costello, Moe Dalitz, Detroit's Purple Gang, the Reinfeld Syndicate, Meyer Lansky, Bugsy Siegel, and Al Capone. The conviction of Chicago's Al Capone in 1931 for tax evasion was a wake-up call for mobsters. So much money was being illegally earned that it wasn't possible to launder it through car washes and laundromats. New methods had to be found to conceal the sources of illicit money and wash it clean.

The New York gangster Meyer Lansky is widely acknowledged as the architect of offshore money laundering. In his lifetime, Lansky was one of the most powerful crime figures in the United States; he was the inspiration for the Hyman Roth character in the film *The Godfather*. Associates said that Lansky possessed a formidable intellect and an exceptional mastery of numbers. Despite determined efforts by U.S. authorities to build a criminal case against him, he spent little time in jail and after a long and rewarding career retired to a comfortable home in suburban Florida.[4]

Lansky and his partners were underworld entrepreneurs. During the Prohibition era, they sold bootleg liquor, organized a truck rental company, established bottling plants, and hijacked goods smuggled by other gangs. They even ran an efficient maritime shipping business to transport high-quality Scotch across the Atlantic.[5]

Anxious to avoid the fate of Al Capone, Lansky had made his first foray into Swiss banking in the early 1930s, initially with the Exchange and Investment Bank of Geneva and later with the equally shady International Credit Bank of Switzerland.[6] It was Lansky who pioneered the "loan-back" technique. Money was moved in the form of cash, traveller's cheques, or bearer bonds for deposit in numbered Swiss accounts. The money then returned home in the form of "loans" to the person who had initiated the cycle, who would repay the loan with interest, deducting the interest from his taxable income as a business expense.[7] Multinational corporations continue to use a variant of this scheme to reduce their tax obligations.

Lansky saw Canada's potential as a money laundering conduit as early as the 1930s and promoted the repatriation of Mob money through Canada. Years later, he convened a meeting in Mexico with mobsters from Ontario and Quebec to discuss laundering through Canada. The RCMP reported that Mob money was being invested in every kind of business in Toronto, from hotels, restaurants, and shopping plazas, to real estate. Canada had its own Lansky-like figure in William Obront, the financial brains of Montreal's Cotroni crime family, who laundered millions in profits from securities fraud, gambling, prostitution, extortion, and drug trafficking.[8]

When Prohibition ended in 1933, Lansky moved into illegal gambling, initially in New York and Florida. In 1937, he began gambling operations in Batista's Cuba. Cuba soon became an offshore money-laundering centre for the Mob as illicit money arrived in suitcases from the American mainland for transfer elsewhere. In return for kickbacks from casino earnings, Batista made Lansky his official adviser on gambling. In the 1950s, Lansky built the Havana Riviera, a luxurious 440-room hotel and casino. He made a fortune in Cuba but lost everything in 1959 when a small band of revolutionaries led by Fidel Castro overthrew the Batista regime.

Lansky moved offshore again to the Bahamas, a British colony, and began to rebuild a gambling empire. One of his close associates was John Pullman, a skilful fraudster from Canada. As Lansky and his Mob associates developed their enterprises, a new bank opened in Nassau, the Bank of World Commerce, with John Pullman as a director and later president. Soon the International Credit Bank of Switzerland also opened a branch in the Bahamas. Illicit profits were rerouted into legitimate businesses, thus securing the Mob's foothold in banks, brokerage houses, and insurance firms as well as in real estate.[9] Lansky scrupulously filed his U.S. income tax returns every year, declaring his income from legal sources.

As early as 1937, U.S. officials were expressing alarm that wealthy Americans were evading taxes by establishing personal holding companies in the British colonies of the Bahamas and Newfoundland.[10] As the Mob developed their activities in the Bahamas, some British officials expressed concern that the offshore industry would bring renewed protests from the U.S. government. The British authorities, however, did nothing. When Lynden Pindling was elected as Premier of the Bahamas in 1967 on a platform hostile to gambling and corruption, large parts of the offshore industry moved to the nearby Cayman Islands, a British Overseas Territory. Within a few months, money began to pour into Grand Cayman.[11] The first foreign bank to set up shop there was Barclays of the United Kingdom, followed by the Royal Bank of Canada, the Canadian Imperial Bank of Commerce, and the Bank of Nova Scotia Trust Company.[12] Despite warnings from officials, the British government again did nothing and allowed the Cayman Islands to develop into one of the world's most notorious sinks for corrupt money.

There are several explanations for the British government's reluctance to prohibit the development of secrecy jurisdictions on its own territories. By the 1950s and 1960s, the British Empire was collapsing and along with it the wealth that had sustained Britain for centuries. Many colonists and business people in the newly independent countries wanted to take their money out and needed clandestine means to do so. Nicholas Shaxson also suggests that British interests were determined to preserve London's dominant role in international finance and set out to build a "London-centered web of half-British territories ... that would catch financial business from nearby jurisdictions by offering lightly taxed, lightly regulated and secretive bolt holes for money."[13]

The offshore system proliferated in the late 1950s with the development of the London-based Euromarket, which resulted in the liberalization of capital movements and unregulated loan markets. Shaxson notes that the City of London transformed itself into an "offshore island," servicing businesses that were located elsewhere. The market rippled outwards, initially to the Channel Island havens and then to the Caribbean secrecy jurisdictions, which became Euromarket booking centres, "secretive and semi-fictional way stations . . . where the world's wealthiest individuals and corporations, especially banks, could park their money, tax free and in secrecy."[14]

The history of offshore finance, of course, involves more than bootleggers, mobsters, and British imperial ambitions. Secrecy jurisdictions developed independently in Europe to help wealthy Europeans evade taxes. Switzerland is one of the world's oldest and largest havens for criminal money laundering and tax evasion.[15] Over the years, the gangsters have been replaced by the major international accounting firms and by a "pinstripe infrastructure of professional bankers, lawyers and accountants," who continue to play a key role in shaping and promoting offshore facilities for their clients.[16]

Today there are more than seventy secrecy jurisdictions spread throughout the world. They include the Caribbean havens, the Channel Islands, Cyprus, Andorra, Austria, Luxembourg, Lichtenstein, Switzerland, Singapore, and Hong Kong. The tiny island of Nauru in the South Pacific, with one road and a population of less than 10,000, hosts four hundred "banks" providing laundering services for billions of dollars of flight capital from Russia. But secrecy jurisdictions are not limited to Alpine principalities or to the tropical islands of popular imagination; they also exist at the centre of global finance.

Offshore banks have gone to great lengths to attract the assets of "high net worth individuals." While statistical data on the offshore system is limited, the Tax Justice Network estimates that between $21 to $32 trillion of the financial wealth of the world's richest people is lodged in secrecy jurisdictions, resulting in global tax losses of at least $200 billion every year.[17] In 2009, U.S. prosecutors charged the Zurich-based UBS Bank with helping Americans hide assets from the Internal Revenue Service. UBS paid a $780 million penalty and disclosed 4,450 accounts of American customers. The U.S. investigation also revealed that the Canada Desk of UBS Bank was managing some $5.6 billion on behalf of wealthy Canadians. In 2010, a joint CBC News and *Globe and Mail* investigation uncovered more than 1,700 accounts belonging to Canadians at the Geneva-based HSBC Private Bank.[18] In early 2012, the Wegelin Bank of Switzerland was sold after three of its bankers were charged in New York with conspiring to help American clients conceal more than $1.2 billion from American tax authorities. U.S. officials announced that they were investigating eleven other Swiss banks as well.

Canadian banks have a massive presence throughout the Caribbean, including in some of the most notorious secrecy jurisdictions. Among North American banks, only New York's Citibank has more offshore subsidiaries than Scotiabank. In 2002 the Association for the Protection of Quebec Savers and Investors, along with the British Columbia–based Shareholders Association of Canada (SHARE), pressed the six Canadian banks to examine whether their subsidiaries should remain in tax havens, given the unsavoury role of these jurisdictions. All six banks pleaded innocent of any wrongdoing and carried on business as usual.[19] A study by the Université du Québec à Montréal estimated that between 1991 and 2003, the five major Canadian banks avoided $16 billion in provincial and federal taxes through the use of offshore subsidiaries.[20]

Half of all international bank lending and at least half of all global trade on paper is conducted through secrecy jurisdictions, enabling multinational corporations to allocate profits to low-tax jurisdictions and costs to high-tax jurisdictions. Secrecy jurisdictions host more than two million "international business corporations," usually little more than shell companies with a postal address. The British Virgin Islands, with a population of 25,000, hosts an estimated 460,000 business corporations.[21] One modest building in the Cayman Islands is home to more than 18,000 of these entities. Before being exposed as a spectacular fraud, Enron had more than 6,500 shell companies, 600 of which were registered in the Cayman Islands. A December 2008 report from the U.S. Government Accountability Office revealed that 83 of the 100 largest publicly traded companies in the United States, including big banks that received bailout money, have scores of offshore subsidiaries.[22]

Many of the world's largest and most profitable corporations pay little or no tax at all. The U.S.-based Citizens for Tax Justice has calculated that between 2006 and 2011, General Electric's net federal income taxes were *negative* $2.7 billion, despite $39.2 billion in pre-tax American profits over the period.[23] In a technique called the "Dutch sandwich," Google cut its tax rate by more than US$3 billion by channelling profits through Ireland, the Netherlands, and Bermuda.[24] Profitable American companies with offshore subsidiaries that paid no federal taxes in 2010 included Bank of America, Exxon/Mobil, Boeing, and Citicorp.[25] A March 2012 investigation reported that thirty large American companies that paid no federal income tax between 2008 and 2010 were major contributors to American political leaders in both parties – particularly to the committee members that control tax policy in both chambers of Congress.[26]

A U.S. Senate investigation estimated that tax evasion costs the United States $100 billion annually.[27] British tax expert Richard Murphy has calculated that the annual loss to the UK treasury is at least £70 billion.[28] Canada's auditor general warned in 2002 that corporate "tax arrangements with foreign affiliates have eroded Canadian tax revenues of hundreds of millions of dollars over the past 10 years."[29] One-quarter of all of Canada's investments overseas are now going to known tax haven countries, according to a 2012 Statistics Canada report. That amounted to $165 billion in 2011 alone.[30]

Tax evasion and capital flight have even more serious consequences for developing countries. A Washington-based group, Global Financial Integrity (GFI), found that between 2000 and 2008, developing countries lost an average of $725 billion to $810 billion per year, almost ten times what they received in international aid, largely due to commercial tax evasion.[31] In a 2011 report on Africa, GFI calculated that between 1970 and 2008, Africa lost at least $854 billion from illicit financial flows. GFI noted that this was likely an underestimate and that the magnitude of African illicit outflows during this period could be as high as $1.8 trillion.[32]

These findings on Africa are corroborated by other studies. Ndikumana and Boyce found that $700 billion fled thirty-three sub-Saharan countries between 1970 and 2008.[33] This means that sub-Saharan Africa is a net creditor to the rest of the world, its foreign assets far exceeding its foreign debts of $175 billion. Most of these assets are in the hands of private individuals; in 2007, African "high net worth individuals" held $1 trillion in offshore accounts.[34] Ndikumana and Boyce have estimated that debt service payments on loans that fuelled capital flight have resulted in more than 75,000 additional infant deaths annually in the sub-Saharan region.[35]

A 2009 study commissioned by Christian Aid (UK) calculated that trade mispricing by transnational enterprises costs the world's forty-nine poorest countries $160 billion a year in lost tax revenues.[36] GFI looked at illicit capital flight from forty-eight least-developed countries (LDCs); it found that between 1990 and 2008, $197 billion flowed out of these LDCs, mainly into developed countries.[37] Pak, de Boyrie, and Nelson found that commodities trading between thirty African countries and the United States from 2000 to 2005 resulted in Africa losing over $13 billion to the U.S. owing to trade mispricing.[38]

The World Bank and the UN Office on Drugs and Crime (UNDOC) estimate that developing countries lose $20 to $40 billion each year through corruption, with most of that money channelled through secrecy jurisdictions.[39] During his tenure, Nigerian dictator Sani Abacha looted $3 to $5 billion, which was laundered through the United Kingdom, Switzerland, Lichtenstein, Jersey, and the Bahamas. Indonesia's Suharto looted $15 to $35 billion, Mobutu of Zaire $5 billion. Marcos of the Philippines stole an estimated $5 to $10 billion, of which only $624 million was recovered through the Stolen Assets Recovery initiative (StAR).[40] The StAR initiative estimates that only $5 billion in stolen assets have been repatriated to developing countries over the past fifteen years.

These data clearly show that developing countries' economies are being deprived of vast amounts of potential investment capital and that their governments are being denied the tax revenues they need to support health services, education, shelter, social security, and public infrastructure. Countries that lose the ability to raise their own resources become more dependent on foreign aid – this, at a time when aid levels are shrinking. As the Tax Justice Network has pointed out, the loss of tax revenues is heightening inequality and poverty, corroding democracy, and obstructing economic growth.[41] Raymond Baker calls the hemor-rhage of resources from poor countries the "ugliest chapter in global eco-nomic affairs since slavery."[42]

o o o

"The era of banking secrecy is over," proclaimed the 2009 official commu-niqué of the G20 meeting in London.[43] G20 leaders, presiding over the worst economic recession in a generation, recognized that the shadow banking system had contributed heavily to the economic crisis that began in 2008. G20 leaders vowed to crack down on the offshore system, threatening to deploy sanctions against non-cooperative jurisdictions, including tax havens. The communiqué announced that the Organiza-tion for Economic Co-operation and Development (OECD) would imme-diately publish a list of jurisdictions that were not in compliance with OECD standards on transparency and exchange of information for tax purposes.

The OECD list, released on the same day as the G20 communiqué, was divided into three sections: a "blacklist" of non-compliant states, a "grey list" of jurisdictions that had committed to but not yet met the standards, and a "white list" of those substantially in compliance. Aston-ishingly, within days of the close of the G20 meeting, the black zone was empty. Intense diplomatic pressure had succeeded in removing the most notorious secrecy jurisdictions from the blacklist.

Since the 2009 meeting in London, G20 leaders have continued to identify the lack of regulation in the financial system as problematic, but the language on secrecy has all but disappeared. Subsequent OECD initia-tives to tackle harmful tax competition have proven to be largely ineffec-tive. Christensen and others have criticized the OECD's model Double Taxation Agreements (DTAs) and Tax Information Exchange Agreements (TIEAs) as essentially useless since they are bilateral treaties in which information exchange is usually done upon request.[44] This means that tax authorities must have already investigated and constructed a case against an individual before requesting additional information. Moreover, even if there is an agreement to exchange information, it may not be available. In some cases this is quite deliberate.

In response to the lacuna in international action, the Tax Justice Network has launched a "Financial Secrecy Index" that ranks countries according to their level of secrecy and the scale of their financial activities.[45] The index assesses a country's laws and regulations and international treaties as well as their size and importance to global financial markets. In the 2011 assessment, the top 5 out of 71 jurisdictions were Switzerland, the Cayman Islands, Luxembourg, Hong Kong, and the United States. The index showed that the world's most secretive jurisdictions are largely wealthy nations and that many are members of the OECD as well as the G20.

The Financial Secrecy Index also reveals that mainstream thinking about the politics and geography of corruption is seriously flawed. Transparency International ranks some of the world's major secrecy jurisdictions, such as Switzerland, Luxembourg, the United States, and the United Kingdom, as among the "least corrupt." Yet Switzerland's banks have provided services to drug dealers and criminals, including the Cali cartel, the Medellin cartel, the Russian Maffiya, the Sicilian Mafia, and a crowded gallery of corrupt dictators.[46] In the United States, it is perfectly legal for financial institutions to handle the proceeds of a lengthy list of crimes as long as those crimes are committed elsewhere. Moreover, the tiny state of Delaware is one of the world's largest secrecy jurisdictions, home to thousands of shell companies and holding an estimated $5 trillion in undeclared assets.[47] Almost half of the world's secrecy jurisdictions are connected to the UK as Crown Dependencies, British Overseas Territories, or members of the Commonwealth. Christensen argues that there is a need to draw public attention to the people and institutions that comprise the "supply-side" of corruption.[48]

Civil society organizations such as the Tax Justice Network, Global Financial Integrity, OXFAM-UK, Global Witness, Christian Aid (UK), the Halifax Initiative, and labour movements have been joined by dozens of citizens' groups worldwide to promote global financial transparency, especially on tax matters, among governments and multilateral institutions. Key among CSO demands is the establishment of a multilateral framework for the automatic exchange of tax information. Such a multilateral agreement would require governments to collect from financial institutions data on income, gains, and property paid to non-resident individuals, corporations, and trusts. This would be a much more robust approach compared to the OECD's weak bilateral models of information exchange "on request."

CSOs have also been campaigning for the adoption of international accounting standards requiring multinational corporations to report sales, profits, and taxes paid on a country-by-country basis in their audited annual reports and tax returns. Currently most multinationals report only consolidated accounts, which makes it impossible to determine where companies are working, how many employees they have in each geographic location, and the amount of taxes they remit to host governments. Country-by-country reporting would require information on sales, purchases, labour costs, financing costs, pre-tax profits, tax charges, costs, and value of assets. CSOs have made representations to the International Accounting Standards Board to promote the adoption of this standard. Not surprisingly, this proposal is being actively resisted by multinational companies, for it would limit their ability to shift profits and taxes across jurisdictions.

CSOs are also advocating that the UN Committee of Experts on International Co-operation on Tax Matters be strengthened in terms of mandate and resources. The G77 group of developing countries and China have proposed that the UN tax committee be upgraded to an intergovernmental commission – a position that the OECD, which includes Canada and the European Union – adamantly opposes. However, the UN is far better able to represent the interests of developing countries than the OECD, which is largely a club of rich countries, and which, as we have seen, has serious credibility problems in this area.

CSOs are also promoting the integration of responsible tax policies into corporate accountability frameworks. Corporate integrity and good practice mean complying not merely with the letter of the law but also with its spirit. Taxes are a key aspect of how corporations relate to the societies that nurture them. Tax revenues pay for the goods and services on which corporations depend – public infrastructure, access to the environmental commons, an educational system that trains workers, social and health services, significant subsidies, and a complex and costly legal system that safeguards corporate contracts and property rights. Tax expert Richard Murphy argues that tax is not a business cost. Rather, tax is much like a *dividend* – a return due on investments made by society-at-large, and derived from the "commons," from which corporations benefit.

Ultimately, what is required is a change of attitudes about the role of taxation in our societies. Taxes are a crucial part of the democratic social contract between citizens and the state. Yet political leaders of all stripes typically refer to taxes as a burden, rather than the way we have collectively organized to provide the infrastructure and services enjoyed by everyone. When wealthy citizens and commercial actors opt out of taxation, the social contract is undermined and public cynicism prevails. In this context, a public discussion about a fair and progressive tax system is urgently required – a public discussion that might lead to the end of tax evasion as a norm, and to the end of state-sponsored "havens" that expedite such evasion.

Transparency and accountability in the international financial system have been resisted by powerful players and jurisdictions that profit from the status quo. However, as it becomes widely recognized that secrecy spaces have inflicted enormous damage on local economies, citizens' groups are organizing in most parts of the world to resist and transform this reality. Creative public education activities have developed such as the Tackle Tax Havens and the Robin Hood Tax campaigns. Citizens' groups in Africa are mobilizing to demand that their governments engage in transparent negotiations with multinational companies regarding taxation, royalties, and the recovery of social and environmental costs. The Occupy Wall Street movement has focused public attention on the financial system's role in creating and maintaining profound levels of economic inequality not experienced since the 1920s.

This burgeoning movement is achieving a critical mass, locally and globally, and offers the possibility that we might collectively begin to rebuild societies rooted in sound economics and an ethics of responsible citizenship, equality, and social solidarity. There is no better place to start than to eradicate secrecy jurisdictions that allow a few to concentrate obscene levels of wealth while communities – and nations – crumble and the local and global commons erodes and disappears.

5

The Failure of Corporate Tax Cuts to Stimulate Business Investment Spending

JIM STANFORD

Introduction

INVESTMENT IN FIXED CAPITAL ASSETS is a crucial driver of economic growth, job creation, technological change, and productivity growth.[1] In a capitalist economy, most such investment is undertaken by private businesses (although public investment spending plays an important supplementary role in capital accumulation). Hence the vibrancy and success of business investment spending is central to the overall state of the economy.[2] When aggregate investment spending is high as a share of total GDP, economies tend to grow faster, to experience faster productivity improvements,[3] and to generate stronger income growth. This was true in Canada during the 1960s and 1970s (when total national capital spending accounted for over 20 per cent of GDP), and it is true today in high-investment economies such as Korea, China, and Brazil.

Capital spending by business in Canada in recent years has been disappointing. Business spending declined more than any other category of domestic expenditure as Canada entered the recession of 2008–09. Yet business investment recovered more slowly from the recession than any other category of spending. Indeed, the business sector is the only sector in Canada's economy that was still spending less at the end of 2011 than in autumn 2008, before the recession started. In contrast, consumer spending and government spending both increased substantially (partly as a result of pro-active stimulus efforts, including lower interest rates and discretionary fiscal policy). In short, business investment spending was the major source of Canada's recent downturn, and the slowness of the recovery in business spending is a key reason why Canada's recovery from the recession is still uncertain, sluggish, and incomplete. It is worth noting that this sharp downturn in business investment occurred precisely coincident with another round of reductions in federal corporate income taxes, which were cut by the Harper government from 22.1 per cent in 2007 (including the former 1.1 per cent federal surtax) to 18 per cent by 2010. Whatever impact this 4-point reduction in federal corporate income taxes may have had (or not had) on business investment, it was vastly overwhelmed by other macroeconomic factors, which proved far more important in determining business investment spending.

After being re-elected with a majority in 2011, the Conservatives reduced the rate further (to 15 per cent by January 1, 2012). The government claimed that these cuts would spark increased business investment and thereby generate more jobs and higher incomes for all Canadians. This is at odds with the recent history of Canadian business investment spending: business spending declined substantially, and stayed lower than previous levels, despite the 4-point tax cut implemented between 2006 and 2010. Tax reductions to business are highly regressive in their distributional effects (since most income on capital is received by the wealthiest segments of society), and this has made corporate tax cuts all the more controversial politically.[4] This chapter will evaluate whether there is any longer-run empirical support for the claim that lower corporate taxes elicit more business investment.

Section 1 of the chapter reviews empirical data regarding trends in business investment spending in Canada. This evidence indicates that business investment spending has clearly declined in Canada (by several measures) in the quarter-century since successive federal governments began reforming and reducing corporate income taxes. Section 2 describes the evolution of corporate tax rates, highlighting repeated reductions in corporate taxes since the late 1980s. Section 3 describes how the combination of higher core profitability and lower tax rates has generated a strong increase in corporate cash flows – pushing cash flow up far above business investment spending. The growing gap between strong cash flows and stagnant investment has produced excess corporate savings and cash accumulation. Section 4 presents the results of original statistical research into what shapes business investment spending in Canada. This analysis confirms that corporate tax rates have had no measurable impact on business investment. Section 5 further interprets the results of this statistical analysis; it finds that while corporate tax rates do not seem to directly influence investment spending, they can have an indirect positive effect on investment (experienced via increments to corporate cash flows). However, that indirect impact is small and has weakened over time. The statistical results suggest that Canadian business investment is influenced primarily by GDP growth trends, interest rates, exchange rates, and oil prices; changes in corporate taxes have no measurable effect. These results suggest that government should place more emphasis on stimulating GDP growth (including through a continued expansion of *public* investment). If the goal is to stimulate more business investment spending (and this is a valid and important goal), then the effects of expansionary fiscal measures (including a positive "crowding in" impact on private business spending) are more significant than corporate tax cuts.

Business Investment Spending

Statistics Canada provides several different sources of data regarding business fixed capital spending: its annual surveys of public and private investment intentions and expenditures; its quarterly national income and expenditure accounts, which detail how investment spending by businesses, and governments, contributes to the evolution of overall GDP; and its quarterly and annual surveys of business finances (based on corporate financial reports). These different surveys all reveal a consistent overall finding: namely, the long run rate of business investment spending slowed in Canada beginning in the 1980s and has not rebounded despite repeated episodes of corporate tax reform.

Figure 1 illustrates data from Statistics Canada's annual investment intentions and expenditures survey. During the initial postwar decades, fixed investment spending fluctuated between 16 and 18 per cent of GDP, declining by about 2 percentage points of GDP after the 1980s. It has fluctuated between 14 and 16 per cent of GDP since then. Investment is highly cyclical, rising and falling with the overall state of economic growth.

Figure 1
Business investment spending as share of GDP, 1961–2010

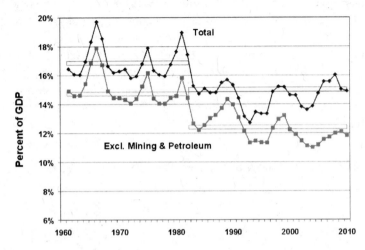

Source: Author's calculations from Statistics Canada, CANSIM data.

In the wake of this long-run slowdown in capital investment, Canada's overall economy has become less capital-intensive in recent decades. This result is counter-intuitive, given the increasing role of technology in our lives and our economy. Businesses are spending less on new capital equipment; moreover, more rapid technological change has meant that existing assets become obsolescent more quickly (and hence depreciation charges are higher). As a result of these two factors, the *net* capital stock (i.e., the stock of fixed capital assets *after* paying for the depreciation of existing equipment) has not kept up with the overall size of Canada's economy.

Most business investment is financed from the internal funds generated by a company's existing operations. A rapidly growing company may turn to the financial markets to raise additional funds for new investment (through loans, bonds, or new equity issues). But the bulk of most companies' new investments (both to replace depreciating assets and to add to the net capital stock) is financed from the funds generated by the company's existing operations.

In fact, the cash flow generated by existing business operations in

Canada is now well in excess of total business spending on non-residential fixed capital. Figure 2 compares fixed non-residential capital spending by businesses with the cash flow that businesses generate from their existing operations. Business fixed non-residential spending averaged between 12 and 13 per cent of GDP during the initial postwar decades[5] and then declined by about one point of GDP after the early 1980s. Initially, the after-tax cash flow of the business sector (equal to before-tax profits, less direct taxes paid to government, plus capital consumption allowances[6]) was broadly equivalent to business investment in non-residential fixed capital.

Figure 2
Business cash flow and investment spending, 1961–2010

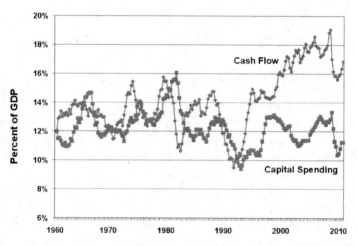

Source: Author's calculations from Statistics Canada, CANSIM data.

Over the past quarter-century, however, the after-tax cash flow received by the business sector in Canada has grown substantially relative to Canada's GDP. This reflects three different components. First, the structural determinants of business profitability have improved markedly in Canada as a result of factors such as stagnant labour compensation, declining unionization, the privatization of formerly public assets, and other policies implemented by successive business-friendly governments. Second, corporate tax rates have been reduced repeatedly and significantly (as will be reported in more detail below). Finally, owing to more rapid technological change and the resulting faster obsolescence of capital, depreciation charges have grown relative to GDP. For all three reasons, after-tax business cash flow has grown since the mid-1980s by 3 to 4 percentage points of GDP.

Since the mid-1980s, therefore, business investment spending has declined, but business cash flow has increased. The result is a growing gap between cash flow and business investment. That gap cumulates to very large sums of uninvested after-tax corporate cash flow – that is, funds received by companies that have *not* been ploughed back into new expenditures on fixed non-residential capital in Canada.[7] From 2001 through 2010 alone, this uninvested cash flow totals to almost $750 billion. Even during the recession (which significantly reduced business profits), uninvested cash continued to flow into corporate coffers. A cumulative total of $200 billion in uninvested cash flow was pocketed by the business sector between the beginning of the recession in the third quarter of 2008 and the end of 2010.

The contrast between stagnant or declining business investment and rising business cash flow is summarized in Figure 3, which illustrates the aggregate reinvestment rate of Canadian businesses. This is the share of after-tax corporate cash flow that is reinvested in new fixed non-residential capital investment. This ratio hovered near 100 per cent during the initial postwar decades. Since the late 1980s, however, it has declined steadily, averaging below 70 per cent through the entire last decade.

Corporate Tax Reductions

Canada has experienced several episodes of business tax reform over the past quarter-century. The first occurred in 1988, under the Progressive Conservative government of Brian Mulroney, when the federal statutory tax rate was reduced from 36 to 28 per cent (not including a 1.1 per cent surtax). At the same time, however, numerous tax loopholes that reduced effective business taxes were closed. The net impact on final taxes paid by business was therefore muted. Then, beginning in 2001, the Liberal government implemented a further reduction in the statutory rate to 21 per cent by 2004. This benefited mainly the services sector of the economy,

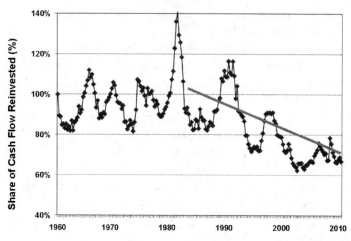

Figure 3
Reinvestment rate, Canada, 1961–2010

Source: Author's calculations from Statistics Canada, CANSIM data.

since the manufacturing and resource sectors had earlier already been paying tax at a favourable 21 per cent rate. Now the overall tax system was supposedly more neutral than before the first reform in 1988. Finally, following the election of a Conservative government under Stephen Harper, the statutory rate was cut again beginning in 2008, reaching 18 per cent by 2010 and falling further, to 15 per cent, by 2012.

At the same time, many provincial governments reduced their own statutory tax rates (often pressed by companies that threatened to relocate their reported profits from one province to another to take advantage of interprovincial tax differences). The combined federal–provincial statutory rate declined from almost 50 per cent in the early 1980s to 29.5 per cent in 2010 and will fall to an estimated 25 per cent if all planned provincial reductions are fully implemented.[8] Combined federal–provincial statutory tax rates will thus have been cut in half by 2013, compared to the early 1980s.

Due to the impact of various deductions and loopholes, the effective tax actually paid by corporations can vary significantly from the theoretical statutory rate. An approximate effective tax rate can be estimated by dividing the sum of direct taxes paid by business by the pre-tax profit base. To reflect the lag times in processing and submitting tax returns, we divide taxes paid by the previous year's before-tax profit.[9] This effective tax rate is almost always lower than the statutory rate. It is interesting to note that the effective tax rate did not decline noticeably following the 1988 tax reform (which simultaneously reduced the rate and closed loopholes, apparently with little net impact on taxes paid). However, the effective rate did begin to decline following the Martin cuts of 2001, gathering pace with the additional across-the-board rate cuts implemented by the Harper government. The Harper rate reductions applied to a broader class of businesses than either of the previous reforms and hence translated more powerfully into a lower effective tax rate.[10]

Table 1
Business profits, taxes, and investment, 1961–2010 (%)

	Tax rates		Business investment		Business profitability		
	Statutory	Effective[a]	As share GDP	As share after-tax cash flow	Pre-tax	After-tax	After-tax cash flow[b]
Pre-reform (1961-1987)	Approx. 50	38.2	12.7	95.3	11.4	6.9	13.4
Mulroney reforms (1988-2000)	42.4	38.1	11.7	89.2	9.5	5.7	13.3
Martin reforms (2001-2007)	35.9	29.3	11.9	68.4	13.7	9.2	17.5
Harper reforms (2008-2010)	30.9	26.5	11.7	69.7	12.2	8.3	16.8
Change from pre-reform to Harper years (in points)	−19.1	−11.6	−1.0	−25.7	+0.9	+1.4	+3.4

Source: Author's calculations from Statistics Canada CANSIM and OECD data, as described in text. Includes private and government business enterprises and fixed non-residential capital spending.

a Effective tax rate is direct taxes on business profits as share of before-tax profits lagged one year.

b After-tax cash flow equals before-tax profits less direct taxes plus capital consumption allowances.

These longer-run developments in business profits, cash flow, income taxes, and capital spending are summarized in Table 1. This table divides the full 50-year period under consideration into 4 sub-periods. The initial postwar decades prior to the major Mulroney reforms of 1988 constitute the first sub-period. Then additional sub-periods are defined according to coverage by each successive set of business tax reforms: the Mulroney, Martin, and Harper reductions.[11]

Table 1 indicates the decline in average statutory and effective tax rates over each period. The statutory rate fell significantly with each reform. The effective tax rate only began to fall significantly with the Martin and then the Harper reductions. Compared to the pre-reform era, the average statutory rate during the Harper reform years (2008 through 2010) was 19 points lower, and the effective rate was 12 points lower.

However, business investment has actually declined relative to the pre-reform period: by 1 full percentage point of GDP in the post-reform period, compared to the pre-reform period. The successive Martin and Harper rate reductions did not affect this performance. During this period, however, after-tax corporate tax flow went up. So measured as a share of available cash flow, investment spending fell more dramatically, by about 25 percentage points (from 95 per cent of cash flow before the reforms to under 70 per cent of cash flow during the Harper reform years).

Components of Corporate Cash Flow

Table 1 also indicates the three components of the increase in after-tax cash flow during this period. Before-tax profits grew by about 1 percentage point of GDP from the pre-reform years to the Harper period.[12] Thanks to lower effective taxes, after-tax profits increased by 1.5 percentage points as a share of GDP. And larger depreciation allowances boosted after-tax cash flow even more substantially: by a cumulative total of some 3.4 points of GDP in the Harper era,[13] compared to the pre-reform era.

As noted, the gap between after-tax corporate cash flow and business fixed non-residential capital spending has given rise to a growing surplus of what we might call "excess corporate saving." Companies are taking in far more cash flow than they allocate to new investments in Canada. This excess saving, which reduces expenditure and purchasing power in the Canadian economy, is especially damaging during times of recession (exactly when the economy needs all sectors to borrow and spend, rather than save and accumulate).

Table 2
Distribution of excess corporate cash flow, 2001–2010 (in billions)

Total uninvested after-tax cash flow	$744.9
Excess accumulation of cash and short-term financial assets[a]	$144.1
Excess dividend payouts[b]	$82.1
Reduction in debt[c]	$232.7
Net outflow of FDI	$89.8
Other (share repurchases, mergers and acquisitions, etc.)[d]	$196.2

Source: Author's calculations from Statistics Canada CANSIM data. Excess cash flow is the cumulative difference between after-tax cash flow (before tax profits less direct taxes plus capital consumption allowances) and fixed non-residential capital spending by businesses, from 2001 through 2010. Includes private and government business enterprises and fixed non-residential capital spending.

a Currency and short-term assets owned by non-financial corporations only, in excess of the average proportion of GDP that prevailed prior to 2001.

b Increase in dividend payouts by businesses above the average share of GDP that prevailed prior to 2001.

c Reduction in corporate debt (short-term, loans, and bonds) as share of total business assets, relative to the ratio recorded at end-2000, times the total value of corporate assets at the end of 2010.

d Residual.

As indicated in Table 2, the cumulative difference between after-tax cash flow and fixed non-residential investment spending by Canadian businesses was $745 billion between 2001 and 2010. What have companies done with all that money? Money is fungible, of course, and can be allocated and reallocated into various compartments, so it is impossible to trace the uses of the actual dollars corresponding to a particular cash flow. We can illustrate, however, some of the alternative uses of cash that companies have undertaken during this era of excess corporate saving. Some of these uses are reported in Table 2.

Companies have notably increased their stockpiles of cash and short-term financial assets. According to Statistics Canada's national balance sheet data, these liquid holdings of non-financial businesses in Canada have increased dramatically as a share of GDP since 2001.[14] That increase in cash holdings (measured relative to the pre-2001 average ratio to GDP) is equivalent to $144 billion through the end of 2010.[15] Dividend payouts to shareholders have also increased (again measured as a share of GDP) relative to pre-2001 averages; this corresponds to an excess cumulative payout of dividends of some $82 billion through to the end of 2010. Companies have substantially reduced their debt (short-term debt, loans, and bonds) relative to their total assets; this is known as business "deleveraging," and it was an important factor in the contraction in credit conditions that accompanied the recent recession. The decline in business debt as a share of total assets since the end of 2000 is equivalent to $233 billion worth of debt repayment through the end of 2010. On a net basis, foreign direct investment (FDI) left Canada over this period (despite the massive increases in FDI associated with recent takeovers of Canadian resource properties). This outflow of capital to foreign jurisdictions could be ascribed as the end use of another $90 billion of the excess savings. The remaining residual (just under $200 billion) could be attributed to a range of other non-productive uses of corporate cash that are more difficult to measure, including share buybacks (which have become common among companies generating more cash flow than they reinvest), acquisitions and takeovers (which result in a reduction of the equity base), and other activities that may make sense for individual companies but that do not translate into real investment in the Canadian economy.

This attribution of excess cash flow to various end uses is by its nature approximate, given the impossibility of tracing any flow of particular money. It is undeniable, however, that corporate Canada has been consistently taking in far more after-tax cash flow – in part as a result of successive reductions in corporate taxes – than it is reinvesting in Canadian capital spending. In that context, accentuating that cash flow through further tax reductions certainly seems like pushing on a string. It is highly likely that these tax reductions have only added to the large sums of uninvested cash flow already being received by Canadian businesses.

Econometric Analysis of Business Investment and Business Tax Rates

To cast some independent light on the significance (or not) of business taxes in the determination of business investment, this section uses statistical techniques to analyze historical data regarding Canadian business investment spending and its potential determinants. We will report the results of several econometric regressions. This involves analyzing statistical data on business investment and its potential causes, in order to examine the apparent strength of possible relationships between them. A strong apparent causal relationship is considered "statistically significant" if analysis indicates it is highly unlikely that the relationship could have appeared by chance.[16] For each of the econometric specifications described and tested below, regressions were conducted both for the entire period for which complete Statistics Canada data on investment are available (1961 through 2010), and then separately for the pre-reform and post-reform periods (before and after 1988, when the Mulroney government implemented the first of several subsequent initiatives to reform and reduce business taxes). This approach allows us to test whether the relationship between taxes and investment (if any) became more or less apparent after this business-friendly shift in taxation policy was adopted beginning in 1988.

Two broad approaches were taken in this statistical analysis. First, we tested for any direct relationship between investment and corporate tax rates by performing simple single-variable regressions of investment (measured by the share of investment in total GDP) on taxes. We consider whether either statutory rates (combined federal–provincial average) or effective rates (calculated as an effective proportion of pre-tax profits) seem to predictably influence investment.

Table 3 summarizes the findings of these simple regressions. There is no robust evidence of a direct relationship between tax rates and business investment. The effective tax rate was not significant in any of the three regressions (total sample, pre-reform, and post-reform). The statutory rate was weakly significant[17] with the expected negative sign[18] in the full sample period, but not in either of the truncated samples.

This simple single-variable approach may miss some of the potential impact of tax rates on investment spending, however, by failing to

Table 3
Tests for significance of tax variables in regressions of business fixed non-residential investment

	Full sample period (1961:1–2010:4)	Pre-reform (1961:1–1987:4)	Post-reform (1988:1–2010:4)
Simple regressions			
Effective tax rate	None	None	None
Statutory tax rate	None	None	10% level (negative)
Multiple regressions (fully specified model[a])			
Effective tax rate	5% level (positive)	None	None
Statutory tax rate	None	None	10% level (positive)

Source: Author's calculations based on Statistics Canada CANSIM and OECD data, as described in text. Dependent variable is first difference of business fixed non-residential capital spending as share of GDP. Full regression results reported in Stanford (2011).
a Coefficients of fully specified model are reported in Table 4.

consider the other major determinants of business investment. So we can also consider the significance of taxes (both statutory and effective rates) in the context of a more complete economic model of business investment. Based on previous econometric research, we considered the following potential causes of investment in our multi-variable regressions:

- *The rate of growth of real GDP.* Business capital spending depends strongly on the growth path of the overall economy. Investment causes growth (known as the "multiplier" effect), and stronger growth in turn generates still more investment (called the "accelerator" effect), because business capacity can become tight, and firms' expectations of future sales become more optimistic.
- *After-tax business cash flow.* This captures both incentive effects (higher profitability likely elicits more investment) and the fact that stronger cash flow makes it easier for businesses to finance investment.[19]
- *Real interest rates.*[20] Higher interest rates undermine business invest-

ment by making it more expensive to finance new projects and by heightening the relative appeal of purely financial investments.

- *Oil prices.* Given the importance of energy-related projects in Canada's overall investment (especially in recent years), oil prices may have an impact on investment spending.
- *The exchange rate.* The international value of Canada's dollar may impact investment spending in complex and contradictory ways, by affecting the cost of imported capital equipment, the cost-competitiveness of Canadian investment locations, and other channels.[21]
- *Capital goods prices.* Some economists[22] have theorized that the decreasing cost of some types of capital equipment (especially information technology) has stimulated more investment.
- *Foreign direct investment inflows and outflows.* Various hypotheses have been advanced regarding the positive impact of inward FDI on total real capital investment in Canada, and the potential negative or positive impacts of outward FDI on domestic investment.[23]
- *Labour costs.* We can measure labour compensation relative to productivity by labour's share of total GDP. This variable may supplement cash flow as an indicator of the structural profitability of business.
- *Control variables.* We also consider the impact on investment of the dramatic events of 1981–82 (the interest rate shock), 2001 (the 9/11 attacks), and 2008–09 (the financial crisis).

Table 4 summarizes the results of this more complete analysis of business investment. The first five causal variables listed above were found to be strongly statistically significant, with the expected effects. The capital goods price index, FDI, and unit labour costs were not significant. The coefficient on real GDP growth indicates relatively strong multiplier and accelerator effects on investment decisions (proving that "growth begets growth"). The coefficient on after-tax cash flow in the full-period regression indicates that on average, something close to 20 per cent of incremental cash flow is reinvested in additional projects.[24] It is noteworthy, however, that the relationship between cash flow and investment weakened by about half in the post-reform period (consistent with the evidence reported above of a widening gap between cash flow and investment spending). The exchange rate variable demonstrated a complex impact on investment: positive initially (perhaps due to correlation

Table 4
Coefficients of the fully specified regression model

Explanatory variables	Lag structure	Sum of coefficients	Single or joint statistical significance[a]	Sum of coefficients	Sum of coefficients
		Full sample period (1961:1–2010:4)		Pre-reform (1961:1–1987:4)	Post-reform (1988:1–2010:4)
Constant	n.a.	–0.0005	not sig.	–0.0004	–0.0009
Change in log of real GDP	1	0.0782	1%	0.0686	0.1252
Change in after-tax cash flow[b]	4,8	0.1714	1	0.2031	0.1001
Change in real interest rate	0,8	–0.000724	5	–0.001050	–0.000242
Change in oil price	1,4	.000210	1	.000379	.000174
Change in exchange rate	0,1,2	–0.00440	5	0.01932	–0.01089
Control variables:					
1981	n.a.	–0.0079	1	–0.0087	n.a.
2001		–0.0068	5	n.a.	–0.0063
2009		–0.0050	5	n.a.	–0.0040

Source: Author's calculations based on Statistics Canada CANSIM and OECD data, as described in text. Dependent variable is first difference of business fixed non-residential capital spending as share of GDP. Full regressions results reported in Stanford (2011).

a Wald test for joint significance of coefficients.

b As share of GDP.

R^{02}: 0.382. Adj. R^{02}: 0.337. S.E. of regression: 0.00278. F-statistic: 8.413. D-W: 1.537.

between the exchange rate and oil prices, or perhaps via the impact of a stronger dollar on the price of imported capital goods), but negative in subsequent years; ultimately a higher dollar has a small net negative impact on investment. Higher oil prices (which increase investment) and higher interest rates (which reduce investment) were both statistically significant.

From this new starting point of a fully specified investment regression, the significance of business taxes can be tested by incrementally including tax rates in the regressions and then seeing if they appear to add any additional insight into the model's explanation of investment. These results are summarized in the lower half of Table 3. Even with due attention given to the other determinants of investment, the tax rate variables do not play their expected explanatory roles. The effective tax rate is significant at the 5 per cent level in the full time period (1961 through 2010) but with a *positive* sign (implying that higher effective taxes elicit *more* investment). This finding does not make intuitive sense; it is probably capturing an indirect correlation of higher effective taxes with stronger profits and/or economic growth. The effective tax rate variables are not significant in either of the two smaller sub-samples. Similarly, the statutory tax variable is weakly significant in the post-reform regression, but again with a *positive* sign; it is not significant in either the full-sample or the pre-reform regressions.

On the basis of both the simple and the multi-variable regressions, therefore, there is no evidence in the Canadian historical data that business tax rates have any significant, measurable influence on business investment spending. Hence the claim that cutting business tax rates will inspire companies to invest more in capital projects in Canada is not supported by real historical experience.

Direct and Indirect Impacts on Investment Spending

Even though there is no evidence of a direct relationship between tax rates and investment, tax policy may still affect investment indirectly via its impact on after-tax cash flow. We saw above that incremental business cash flow tends to be associated positively with investment (with an average reinvestment rate of 20 per cent over the full period, but half that in the post-1988 period). The coefficients for GDP growth and after-tax cash flow from the post-1988 reform regression allow us to simulate the likely impacts of the most recent reduction in business taxes on new investment spending. The cash flow coefficient in the post-reform sample implies that in recent decades, businesses have tended to reinvest only 10 per cent of incremental cash flow in new projects. In the 2011 election campaign, the Harper government proposed a 3-point reduction in corporate tax rates (ultimately costing the federal government some $6 billion per year in forgone revenues – and generating a $6 billion improvement in after-tax business cash flow). According to the coefficient, this new cash flow would translate into new business investment of only $600 million per year; in other words, just ten cents of each dollar in tax savings would be translated into incremental investment spending. The large cash hoards that businesses already carry in Canada further mute the impact of any additional cash flow on incremental investment; hence this prediction, if anything, is likely optimistic.

It is interesting that according to these econometric findings, the federal government would stimulate almost as much *private* business investment by spending the full $6 billion on new *public* investment projects (such as infrastructure construction, public transit, or low-cost housing) instead of reducing business taxes. According to the federal Department of Finance, public infrastructure spending carries a relatively large GDP multiplier effect of 1.6 to 1; this means that each dollar in new public infrastructure investment tends to boost total GDP by $1.60.[25] Many economists have analyzed the "crowding in" effect of government spending on private business capital spending.[26] Public investment can increase private investment thanks to the resulting expansion of the overall economy and also by enhancing the productivity of private enterprise (through better infrastructure). According to the previous regression results, therefore, the *indirect* spinoff impact of $6 billion in new public investment, experienced via the resulting multiplied boost in GDP (of almost $10 billion) on private business spending, would be almost as great ($520 million, according to the coefficients from the post-reform regression) as the direct boost to investment if the government had instead allocated $6 billion to funding the business tax cuts.

However, in this case, the economy also benefits from the initial $6 billion direct increase in public investment. In other words, the *total* increase in investment resulting from a $6 billion allocation to infrastructure ($6.52 billion, public and private) is more than *ten times greater* than the increase in private investment only ($601 million) resulting from a $6 billion allocation to business tax cuts. The reallocation of fiscal "room," therefore, from financing business tax cuts to financing direct public infrastructure investments, would provide a much bigger direct boost to economic growth and job creation – and, perhaps surprisingly, would actually stimulate comparable increases in *private* investment as well.

Conclusion

It is certainly true that fixed capital spending in Canada (both private and public) is an essential source of spending power, job creation, and productivity growth. It is also clear that business investment spending has declined in recent decades and is presently inadequate relative to Canada's need for more capital. Business investment fell deeply during the recent recession and has recovered slowly and incompletely. The issue is what is the best way to stimulate more of this crucial economic activity. Historical evidence regarding the effects of successive rounds of business tax reductions (in 1988, 2001, and since 2007 under the Harper government) does not support the claim that tax reductions provide a major boost to business capital spending.

Particularly given the growing divergence between after-tax cash flow and business non-residential capital spending, and the resulting accumulation of uninvested cash in the bank accounts of Canadian non-financial corporations, additional reductions in corporate tax rates are like "pushing on a string." On the basis of the evidence assembled here, governments would have a more direct and powerful impact on investment spending (both private and public) by emphasizing direct increases in expenditure (directed especially at public capital and infrastructure expansion) rather than additional tax reductions for businesses. Further cuts to business taxes have been both economically ineffective and distributionally regressive.

6

Financial Transaction Taxes

The Battle for a Small but Important Tax

TOBY SANGER

EVEN WHILE GOVERNMENTS SLASH public services and impose austerity measures, the banking and financial sectors that caused the 2008 meltdown have emerged relatively unscathed. Profits and executive pay have rebounded, and now that regulatory reforms have been beaten back, even the most reputable firms are engaging in highly speculative activities, causing more economic instability.

It should be no surprise that a key demand heard in protests around the world, from the Occupy Movement to the 2012 anti-austerity protests across Europe and North America, has been for governments to introduce financial transactions taxes (FTTs).

The financial and economic crisis that began in 2008 led to a long overdue re-evaluation of the financial industry – and to a strong revival of interest in taxing that industry. FTTs are attractive for a number of reasons:

1. They can generate significant revenues at the national and international levels, which can go to pay some of the costs of the financial crisis and to generate funds for development.
2. They can reduce excessive financial speculation and activity, steer more resources into productive investments, and reduce the risk of further financial crises; in short, they can be good for the economy.
3. They are highly progressive, since they are paid almost entirely by the financial sector and by wealthy individuals, and thus reduce inequality.

A grassroots campaign led by anti-poverty and international development activists for a broad-based global FTT has gained the support of Nobel-winning economists, business leaders (such as Bill Gates and Warren Buffett), faith leaders (including the Vatican and the Archbishop of the Anglican Church), and political leaders.

Now that calls to increase the taxes paid by the finance sector have gained more support, powerful opponents in the political and financial world have heightened their criticisms of it. Opposition is especially strong in countries such as the UK, Canada, and the United States, where there are especially close connections between politicians and the finance industry.

German Chancellor Angela Merkel, French President François Hollande, and other European leaders have campaigned in support of an FTT. However, the European Commission's proposal for a 0.1 per cent European FTT has encountered strong opposition from British Prime Minister David Cameron as well as ongoing attacks by Canadian Finance Minister Jim Flaherty.

Opponents of FTTs have criticized them for a number of reasons. One is that they are new, unworkable, and risky. Actually, FTTs are none of those things.

FTTs Are Well Established and Widely Used

One of the oldest of the existing FTTs is Britain's Stamp Duty Tax. This was introduced more than three hundred years ago, in 1694, during the reign of William and Mary. Today it collects around £3 billion (or US$5 billion) a year for the British Treasury from a 0.5 per cent tax on stock transactions.

More than forty countries around the world collect FTTs, thereby generating significant revenues. These countries include economically dynamic ones like Switzerland, Finland, Brazil, China, India, Hong Kong, and Taiwan. The Swiss levy a tax on stock and bond transactions. China levies a tax on stock trades, adjusting the rate in order to cool down or heat up its stock market. Taiwan taxes not only stock and bond transactions but also transactions of financial derivatives such as options and futures (albeit at lower rates). Many more countries levied FTTs in the past before eliminating them during the 1990s, on the eve of the stock market boom that ended in the 2008 financial crisis.

Given all this, there is no question that FTTs are feasible. Indeed, they are an effective way to raise significant revenues at low administrative costs without much economic disruption.

A Strong Economic Case for FTTs

The economic argument for FTTs was first articulated by John Maynard Keynes, the greatest economist of the twentieth century. In 1936, during the Great Depression, he wrote in his "General Theory" that "the introduction of a substantial government transfer tax on all transactions might prove to be the most serviceable reform available, with a view towards mitigating the predominance of speculation over enterprise in the United States."[1]

Many other notable economists have made the case for FTTs. These include the Nobel Prize–winning economist James Tobin, who in 1972 proposed an international tax on currency transactions (the "Tobin Tax") "to throw sand in the wheels" of international finance, reduce speculation, and cushion exchange rate fluctuations.[2] More recently, other Nobel-winning economists, including Joseph Stiglitz and Paul Krugman, have joined more than 1,000 other respected economists in urging governments to introduce FTTs on a global basis.

It is important to recognize that economists who support FTTs do so mainly because they can stabilize economies and promote productive investments, rather than because of the revenues they raise or because they promote social equity. In financial terms, they would play a role similar to that of "sin taxes," which reduce alcohol and tobacco consumption, and environmental taxes, which are designed to reduce pollution and other environmentally degrading activities.

The Recent Financial Crisis and the Global Campaign for FTTs

Current proposals for FTTs go beyond taxing transactions of currencies and stocks and call for them to cover a much broader range of financial instruments, including derivatives. Trading of financial derivatives has increased exponentially in recent decades with very little regulatory oversight. That trading is seen as partly responsible for the severity of the recent financial crisis.

Some have argued that the exponential growth in derivatives trading – in futures, options, swaps, and so on – has magnified financial instability instead of reducing volatility. The value of financial derivatives outstanding now amounts to more than ten times the value of annual global economic output. Clearly, much of this involves investments designed to increase profits through leverage and risky speculation rather than to insure underlying investments against economic fluctuations (which was supposed to be the original purpose of hedging and derivatives).

Financial derivatives have been largely unregulated, and little has been done to contain their growth. Only a few countries tax transactions of financial derivatives (though many do tax other goods and services). The growth in derivatives and in the associated hedge funds, private equity firms, and tax havens has siphoned revenues from national governments and made those governments more vulnerable to the power of financial capital, as countries from Asia to Europe have discovered.

There should be little surprise that support for increased taxation of the financial sector comes from across the political spectrum: new taxes on finance would help to pay down the costs of the recent crisis and to fund social and environmental programs around the world; those taxes would also tame the financial industry and help prevent future financial crises.

The global campaign for broad-based FTTs calls for a tax of a fraction of a per cent on all transactions of stocks, bonds, options, futures, and other financial derivatives – but not on regular bank transactions.

The specific proposal for a Robin Hood Tax has been spearheaded by a coalition of development, environmental, anti-poverty, and labour organizations. Because much of the trading in financial derivatives and foreign currencies is global and highly mobile, FTTs on these would be more effective if established through global or multilateral agreements; but the lack of global agreement should be no impediment to having FTTs introduced at a regional or national level.

Advocates of FTTs propose that half the funds thereby raised be allotted to reducing world poverty and fighting climate change, with the other half earmarked for domestic priorities. This could lead to a win–win–win outcome of reduced economic instability, stronger economic growth, and reduced inequality.

If FTTs were combined with stronger regulation of tax havens, they could also reduce revenue leakage, thereby lowering developing countries' dependence on foreign aid.

Progress – and Opposition – at the International Level

The campaign for FTTs received a boost when the G20 leaders agreed at the Pittsburgh Summit of September 2009 that the "financial sector should make a fair and substantial contribution" towards paying some of the costs of the financial crisis. Those costs continue to escalate: with the deficits of G20 countries increasing by many trillions a year, citizens are bearing the costs through public spending cuts, austerity measures, and consumption tax increases.

In advance of the G20 Summit in Toronto, the International Monetary Fund followed up on that commitment with practical advice for taxing the financial sector. The IMF was undermined, however, by Canadian Finance Minister Jim Flaherty, who loudly opposed FTTs, claiming that such taxes would lead to "excessive, arbitrary or punitive regulation" of the financial sector.[3] Just before the G20 meeting in Toronto, the Harper government sent its ministers on an intense, unprecedented, and ultimately successful campaign to foreign capitals around the world to derail proposals for a global agreement on financial taxes at the G20.

The Canadian government's recent obstructionist role on this issue is an unfortunate reversal of the international leadership role that Canada had previously played. In March 1999, Canada's House of Commons passed a motion stating "that, in the opinion of the House, the government should enact a tax on financial transactions in concert with the international community." Finance Minister Paul Martin and most of the Liberal Party, then in power, supported the opposition NDP, which proposed the motion, while the Conservatives opposed it. Canada's Conservative government is now a ringleader of international opposition to FTTs.

Despite the lack of progress at the G20 level, European countries have moved forward. With strong support from Angela Merkel and former French President Nicolas Sarkozy, a proposal for a Europe-wide FTT was endorsed by the European Commission, which called for an FTT to be introduced across Europe by 2014. Momentum grew in 2011 when both the Vatican and Bill Gates expressed support for a global FTT.

Most of the EU's twenty-seven member nations support an FTT, but strong opposition by a few, including the UK and Sweden, had prevented its adoption at the EU level. However, in 2012, the European Parliament voted overwhelmingly in support of eleven member countries of the EU (representing two-thirds of the EU's GDP) to proceed with implementing an FTT using the EU's process of "enchanced co-operation."

Opposition by some hasn't prevented individual countries from moving forward. The newly elected French president, François Hollande, followed through with his election promise, introducing an FTT of 0.2 per cent in August 2012 for trading in stocks of companies with a market value over €1 billion, with a share of revenues going to international development assistance. Hungary introduced a 0.2 per cent FTT in January 2013. Italy, Spain, and Portugal have also announced their intention to proceed with FTTs at the national level.[4]

Potential Revenues from FTTs

Estimates for the potential revenues generated by FTTs vary with the rate, the instruments covered, and the expected impact, but there is no question that such taxes could raise substantial sums.

Existing FTTs, as limited as they are, already generate significant revenues. For example, the UK's Stamp Duty Reserve Tax on share transactions raises around US$5 billion annually. Existing FTTs in other countries generate similar and often even higher revenues.

The European Commission estimates that its proposed 0.1 per cent FTT on stocks and 0.01 per cent rate on financial derivatives would generate €57 billion (or US$77 billion) annually. There's solid research showing that a tax of 0.005 per cent just on transactions of major global currencies could generate more than US$30 billion annually at a low administrative cost, with little impact on markets.[5]

Estimates for Canada show that an FTT of 0.5 per cent on equity transactions would generate more than $4 billion annually, assuming a 50 per cent reduction in trading volumes.[6] Calculations for the United

States show that a broader-based "financial speculation tax" would generate an estimated $150 billion in revenues.[7]

In addition to the revenues, there are other compelling economic arguments for increased taxation of the financial sector.

The financial sector is too big. Whether considered from a critical political-economic or a more conventional neoliberal perspective, there is broad recognition that the financial sector has grown "too big" for the economy's good. A recent IMF report has suggested as much.[8] Finance is an intermediary industry that does not directly produce goods with end-use values for people; instead, it diverts resources from other, more productive areas. Also, the excessive salaries and bonuses paid to financial sector professionals, including many engineering graduates, to create new financial products and derivatives divert those people from work on more fundamental social needs.[9]

Tax changes have strongly favoured the financial sector. Major tax changes introduced in recent decades have greatly benefited the financial sector and those who run it. Those changes, long called for by supply-side economists, include preferential tax rates for capital gains and investment income, cuts to corporate taxes, and reduced taxes for those in the higher tax brackets. These changes have also increased governments' dependence on consumption-based value-added taxes (VATs), such as Canada's GST and HST, that largely exempt financial services. Also, weak regulation and enforcement has allowed the banking and financial industry to avoid taxes through the extensive use of tax havens.

Incentives for excessive risk taking need to be reduced. There is increasing recognition that preferential tax regimes, including lower rates on "investment" income and stock options, have increased the incentives for short-term speculation and excessive risk taking in the financial sector. The IMF and the European Commission have acknowledged this. The laws governing bankruptcy and limited liability have for centuries limited the downside risks for corporations. Since the financial crisis, there has been more focus on the damage caused to the entire economy by systemically risky activities by "too big to fail" financial corporations, which have learned to expect government bailouts.

Despite these compelling arguments, many criticisms and myths about financial transaction taxes persist.

Myths

Myth: *An FTT would harm the economy, reduce economic growth, and increase unemployment.*

Opponents of FTTs claim that they reduce economic growth and increase unemployment. For instance, British Prime Minister David Cameron told the annual World Economic Forum in Davos, Switzerland, that a European FTT would be economic "madness" and result in half a million lost jobs.[10]

In particular, opponents have made wide use of the EC's initial technical impact assessment, which estimates the impact using a highly hypothetical model of the economy. The EC Commissioner for Taxation had admitted that these initial estimates were inaccurate. Since then, the EC has produced revised estimates: it now suggests that that a European FTT would increase GDP by between 0.2 and 0.4 per cent if the revenues were spent on public investment.[11] And these calculations don't include potential positive impacts such as reduced speculation, increased productive investment, and greater stability.

A common criticism of FTTs is that they increase the cost of raising capital by adding to the cost of selling stocks and bonds. Some also argue that higher transactions costs would reduce the efficiency of the free market by reducing liquidity.

However, most FTTs apply only to the secondary trading market for equity shares and bonds. Initial public offers are exempted, so an FTT involves little or no additional cost for those who buy shares as longer-term investments. In any case, most private investment is financed from retained earnings rather than from funds raised in capital markets.

Transaction costs – the costs of buying and selling shares and other financial instruments – have dropped significantly in recent years. Yet there's little evidence that reduced financial transaction costs have increased economic growth. In fact, some results suggest there's a negative relationship: lower transaction costs on equities are associated with lower economic growth.[12]

The reality is that FTTs would have a negligible impact on smaller individual investors, especially those who hold their investments for longer periods. They would have a much greater impact on larger traders who are constantly buying and selling stocks, bonds, and other financial instruments, such as high-frequency traders and day traders – and that's just the point. For smaller investors, FTT costs are likely to be far less than the trading fees charged by banks and investment dealers.

High-frequency trading has been growing rapidly and is now estimated to account for more than half the trading on U.S. stock markets and more than one-quarter of trading in equities on Canadian stock markets.[13] High-frequency traders have much faster access to trading platforms, and this preferential access allows them to exploit price differences and market timing opportunities and to distort markets at the expense of ordinary investors. Some argue that high-frequency trading has strengthened the market by increasing liquidity and reducing price differences. But it has also led to greater market instability – indeed, it was blamed for the "Flash Crash" of 2010.

High-frequency traders and other short-term speculative traders generate much higher profits when there is greater market volatility and a greater imbalance of information, so they welcome developments that increase volatility and the imbalance of information in their favour.

Increased volatility caused by speculators isn't just a concern for financial markets: it can have a very real negative impact on individuals and the economy. For example, oil speculators such as hedge funds and large investment banks such as Goldman Sachs that quickly flip contracts now represent about 70 per cent of the trading in oil contracts – double their share from two decades ago.[14] The Federal Reserve Bank of St. Louis has concluded that speculation played a significant role in oil price increases between 2004 and 2008 as well as in their subsequent collapse.[15] Even Rex Tillerson, CEO of ExxonMobil, and Saudi Arabia, the world's largest producer and exporter of oil, have suggested that speculation is responsible for about 40 per cent of the recent high price of oil.[16]

There's a strong case to be made that FTTs would have a *positive* impact on the economy, not a negative one:[17]

1. They would reduce the role of high-frequency and speculative traders in markets, thereby increasing market stability and economic growth.
2. They would dampen speculation, thereby encouraging investment in productive activities.

3. Revenues raised from FTTs would likely be used in ways that provide a stronger boost to the economy and job growth. For example, public investment almost always has a stronger economic impact than corporate tax cuts.

Myth: *An FTT would tax ordinary transactions, such as deposits, withdrawals, and direct payments.*

Almost all existing FTTs exempt ordinary financial transactions, and none of the FTTs now being considered would affect ordinary retail banking transactions.[18]

The value of retail banking transactions conducted by individuals pales in comparison to the value of financial transactions carried on among banks, dealers, and other financial firms. There is no interest in taxing ordinary banking transactions, since they don't increase financial and economic instability.

Myth: *The costs of an FTT will be paid by ordinary individuals and pensioners.*

Opponents claim that banks and investment dealers will ultimately pass all the costs of FTTs onto ordinary individuals and pensioners through higher fees.

This isn't very likely. Analysis by the European Commission shows that banks and other financial institutions, such as hedge funds, are responsible for 85 per cent of all taxable trades.[19] A large majority of these transactions are conducted on their own accounts or for businesses or very wealthy individuals.

The IMF has analyzed who would end up paying FTTs and has concluded they are "highly progressive": a much higher share would be paid by those with higher incomes, which is not the case with sales taxes, which are regressive.[20]

Some costs might be passed on to ordinary individuals, but these would be far less than what they would pay with other types of taxes. When the benefits of higher public spending and/or reduced taxation in other areas are factored in, the net impact on middle- and lower-income families is invariably positive. And since one of the main goals of FTTs is to reduce speculation and promote productive investments, the longer-term dynamic impact on the economy should also be very positive.

Competition in the industry (where it exists) should limit the degree to which businesses are able to pass on the cost of FTTs to consumers. Where competition is limited, governments as the guarantors and regulators of the banking industry should regulate the fees charged.

Myth: *Banks and financial institutions are already heavily taxed, and an FTT would be excessive, arbitrary, and punitive.*

Canadian Finance Minister Jim Flaherty kicked off his international campaign against FTTs when he claimed that they would result in "excessive, arbitrary, or punitive" regulation of the financial sector.

Banks and financial firms, especially in Canada, have been highly profitable over the past two decades. As the EC background paper on this issue notes, the high profitability of this sector could be the result of higher productivity, lack of competition, the existence of a safety net provided by governments, banking regulations, or tax exemptions.[21]

These high profits can represent "economic rents," whereby firms are able to generate excess profits at the expense of their customers as a result of these factors. There is also evidence of a significant earnings premium for executives in the financial sector – estimated at about 40 per cent – which can represent the presence of these excessive profits. Some financial industry experts suggest that the industry is too large for the economy and that higher profits and compensation packages divert resources from more productive sectors of the economy.

Because of its higher profits, the financial sector has tended to pay a higher-than-average share of domestic corporate income taxes. Yet there's plenty of evidence that banks and financial firms are *undertaxed* compared to other sectors of the economy:

· Comprehensive analysis of the global taxes paid by multinationals indicates that the financial sector pays some of the lowest tax rates compared to other industries.[22] This is because large banks and financial firms are able to exploit tax havens and international taxation rules more than most other industries. Calculations show that Canada's top five banks reduced their Canadian taxes by an average of more than $1 billion annually from 1993 to 2007 by using tax havens and by $2.4 billion alone in 2007.[23]

- Almost all value-added taxes, such as the GST and HST, provide exemptions for most financial services. This tax exemption for financial services provides major benefits to the industry, for it reduces the prices of its services, thus increasing the industry's profits. The benefits of these tax exemptions are shared by the customers of financial service firms – that is, by those with higher incomes. The IMF estimates that the value of this tax exemption for the Canadian financial sector amounts to around $5 billion a year. The exemption of financial services from value-added taxes is a major rationale behind the IMF's proposal to implement a Financial Activities Tax.[24]

- Larger banks and financial firms benefit from the "too big to fail" (TBTF) guarantee that governments implicitly or explicitly provide to big banks to prevent financial crises. TBTF enables large banks and financial firms to engage in risky (and more profitable) activities in the knowledge that they will always be rescued or bailed if they suffer big losses. Calculations of the value of this subsidy guarantee vary with the circumstances, but estimates for the eighteen largest American banks are between $6 to $34 billion for 2009.[25]

- Over the past decade in Canada, the financial sector has been the greatest beneficiary of tax preferences and corporate tax cuts. The annual value of tax savings from lower corporate tax rates since 2001 now amounts to more than $6 billion a year for the finance and insurance sector and to more than $3 billion a year for the banking sector alone. The cumulative tax savings for the finance and insurance sector have amounted to more than $30 billion since 2001.[26] These tax savings do not include the value of tax preferences such as lower tax rates on capital gains and stock options.

New taxes on finance, such as FTTs, would help compensate for inequities like these.

Myth: *FTTs are easily avoided and don't work.*

Opponents of FTTs claim they can be easily avoided and don't work, usually pointing to Sweden's experience with FTTs in the late 1980s.[27]

It's true that Sweden's experiment with FTTs was a failure and simply led to trading in Swedish shares moving offshore, but that's because its tax was poorly designed. Following the example of countries that have successful FTTs in place could minimize this type of avoidance. In particular, FTTs should base their tax on the tax residence of the financial institution or trader, not on where the trade takes place. They should also include the provision that the FTT must be paid in order for change of ownership to be considered legal.

Financial derivatives have been largely unregulated. Most of them are traded "over the counter" between dealers instead of through stock exchanges or centralized clearing systems. However, new rules agreed upon by the Bank for International Settlements and the Financial Stability Board now require transactions involving financial derivatives to be reported through centralized clearing systems.

Centralized clearing systems for financial transactions make it very easy and administratively efficient to collect FTTs. As a result, collection and compliance costs for FTTs are considerably below collection and compliance costs for other types of taxes, including income, sales, and property taxes. As the European Commission notes:

> Taxing financial transactions is one of the least expensive ways of collecting taxes, as most transactions are carried out electronically and the tax can be collected electronically and at the source. FTT can be collected at very low cost (less than 1% of revenue raised), especially when good use can be made of existing market infrastructures, e.g. with the help of trading platforms, trade repositories or clearing houses.[28]

Appropriate design and enforcement of FTTs would limit the benefits and risks of relocation, but those taxes would need to be combined with stricter crackdowns on the use of tax havens.

Myth: *FTTs need to be global to work.*

Some argue that FTTs need to be global in order to work. This partly explains why many politicians offer only qualified support for FTTs, committing to introduce them only if all major nations agree.

While a global agreement on FTTs would be preferable, the lack of such an agreement does not prevent countries from moving forward with them at the national level. More than forty countries – including small nations as well as some of the largest – have domestic FTTs, which is clear evidence that there is no need for such taxes to be global in order to work effectively. Because it is taking some time for EU nations to agree on a European-wide FTT, two countries – France and Hungary – have already moved ahead on their own by introducing FTTs at the national level in 2012 and 2013. Italy and Portugal are also expected to introduce FTTs at the national level in 2013.

For more internationally mobile transactions of foreign exchange and financial derivatives, it would be especially helpful to have a global agreement, but even that is not necessary. While most national FTTs just cover transactions of stocks and bonds, some also cover financial derivatives.

One example of an FTT that would be especially well suited to a global agreement is a currency transaction tax. The Leading Group on Innovative Financing for Development – an organization of more than seventy countries, international organizations, and the Gates Foundation – has recently called for an international tax on currency transactions to fund international development.

Myth: *FTTs would reduce market liquidity and increase economic volatility.*

There has been considerable debate and analysis of the impact of financial transactions taxes on market liquidity and volatility.

It has been hotly debated whether the increased volume, speed, and variety of financial transactions has increased financial volatility and economic uncertainty. At the microeconomic level of individual markets, an increased volume of transactions often leads to *less* volatility and short-term price variation.[29] There's little disagreement that FTTs would reduce the volume and probably also the value of market transactions. A number of studies have also demonstrated a correlation between the introduction or increase in FTTs and greater short-term volatility of equity market prices. This is to be expected, for changes in tax rates add to market uncertainty over the short term. But short-term market volatility isn't the same as broader, long-term financial and economic volatility.

At the same time, financial crises have become both more frequent and more painful in over the past three decades.[30] With the rapid expansion of high-frequency trading and the increased dominance of speculators in many markets in recent years, overall market and economic volatility has also increased.

Before the recent financial crisis, it was thought that the rapid expansion of the financial sector and the development of various types of financial products such as derivatives would result in greater economic stability. Even Ben Bernanke, Chairman of the U.S. Federal Reserve, gave a reassuring speech in 2004 about how this had helped foster the "Great Moderation." It is now understood, however, that this represented a period of false calm before the storm of the financial crisis.[31]

Eric Lascelles, Chief Economist for RBC Global Asset Management, recently concluded that our economies are likely to suffer "ever more bubbles ever more quickly" as a result of increased leverage, speculative trading strategies, and the proliferation of derivatives.[32]

A principal objective of FTTs is to reduce high-frequency speculative trading (which is destabilizing) without impacting longer-term investments. Reduced transactions volumes that provide robust liquidity are better than higher (i.e., speculative) volumes that inflate values until they burst. FTTs would help limit speculative transactions and ensure that market activity is driven more by fundamental economic conditions.[33]

China's system of FTTs goes even further by combining the passive benefits of FTTs with active changes to its stock transactions tax. The latter tax is increased to cool down the stock market when it is getting overheated, then lowered when the market needs a boost.

Myth: *Stronger regulation of the financial industry is preferable to FTTs.*

Some argue that transactions taxes are unnecessary as long as there is effective regulation of the financial sector.

FTTs are no substitute for effective financial regulation. That said, taxes can actually be a good *complement* to regulation. Recall that Al Capone, the infamous American gangster, was ultimately convicted and sent to jail for tax evasion rather than for his role in other criminal activities (including murder).

FTTs could actually improve financial regulation. The 2008 financial crisis convinced G20 financial regulators that they needed much better information on transactions of financial derivatives – which Warren Buffett once called "financial weapons of mass destruction." Those regulators now require that these transactions be conducted through central clearing counterparties. There is also a problem with the growing "dark pools" of capital: alternative trading systems have absorbed 25 per cent of the volume of trades from stock exchanges, including the Toronto Stock Exchange.[34] Requiring payment of a small tax on each transaction would provide governments with much greater enforcement powers.

Some people do not see the growth of unregulated and unmonitored financial transactions as a problem. Meanwhile, though, people around the world are paying the price – in unemployment, lost economic opportunities, bailouts to the financial sector, public and personal indebtedness, and cuts to public services – for decades of lax financial regulation and growing economic imbalances. Those costs now amount to trillions of dollars.

During the financial crisis, G20 leaders promised to require the financial sector make a "fair and substantial commitment" towards paying down the costs of the crisis. Three years later, that commitment remains unfulfilled, largely due to an orchestrated lobbying campaign by Canada's government to sabotage any international agreements on taxation of the financial sector. When Finance Minister Flaherty berated European leaders for pursuing an FTT in the EU, he appeared more concerned about protecting friends in the financial industry than protecting public finances.[35]

G20 leaders also committed themselves to strengthening regulation of the financial sector to help prevent more crises from occurring. There has been little progress on that, either. Highly paid lobbyists from the banking and financial sector have succeeded in watering down attempts at financial reform in the United States. The impact of this watering down was evident in 2012, when J.P. Morgan lost more than $3 billion from trading in derivatives.[36] There has been very little progress on strengthening regulation in other countries either.

FTT implementation is one area where clear and demonstrable progress could be achieved. It would reduce excessive levels of financial speculation; it would also strengthen financial regulation, reduce economic instability, and steer more resources towards productive investments. And it would generate tens of billions of dollars worldwide that could be used to fund social and environmental priorities at home and abroad.

FTTs would not fix all problems with finance, eliminate speculation, or generate enough revenues to address global poverty and environmental challenges. But at a time when governments have reacted to the financial crisis by penalizing people with cuts to public spending, increasing taxes on finance would be much more equitable as well as better for the economy.

It may seem like a win–win–win solution, but there's big money supporting the political opposition to FTTs. That's why popular campaigning is so essential to having this tax introduced.

7

Taxes and Ecological Justice?

JOE GUNN

The tar barons of Alberta have been able to hold the whole country to ransom. They have captured Canada's politics and are turning this lovely country into a cruel and thuggish place. Canada is a cultured, peaceful nation, which every so often allows a band of rampaging Neanderthals to trample all over it. Timber companies were licensed to log the old-growth forest in Clayaquot Sound; fishing companies were permitted to destroy the Grand Banks: in both cases these get-rich-quick schemes impoverished Canada and its reputation. But this is much worse, as it affects the whole world. The government's scheming at the climate talks is doing for its national image what whaling has done for Japan.

The immediate threat to the global effort to sustain a peaceful and stable world comes not from Saudi Arabia or Iran or China. It comes from Canada. How could that be true?
— George Monbiot, in *The Guardian* (UK), November 20, 2009[1]

The country's gone rogue over oil.... Since the late 1990s a bitumen boom, driven by rising oil prices and give-it-away royalties, has created the world's largest energy and engineering project in northern Alberta, a western province home to the Rocky Mountains, cowboys, and boreal forest. As a consequence, Canada now ranks as the world's sixth largest oil producer. Oil lobbyists dominate the nation's capital and bitumen now accounts for more than 30 percent of the nation's exports. Not surprisingly, the nation's embassies lobby against carbon taxes and low-carbon fuel standards abroad with Saudi-like enthusiasm.
— Andrew Nikiforuk, in *Adbusters*, June 26, 2012[2]

ON JUNE 4, 2012, ENVIRONMENTAL ORGANIZATIONS in Canada, along with allied groups, organized a unique, symbolic act of resistance. Frustrated with measures in the federal government's omnibus budget that would "silence" environmental groups, we launched a protest called "Black Out, Speak Out" by darkening our Web pages for a day.

Clearly, thousands of Canadians were worried that Bill C-38, which supposedly outlined taxation and spending measures for the coming year, actually did much more. That bill called for major changes in a multitude of policy areas, including the environment, immigration, and human resources; it also amended dozens of laws. Furthermore, it earmarked $8 million for increased monitoring of environmental charities even while loosening the rules governing environmental assessments for major development projects. More than five hundred organizations, including Canadians for Tax Fairness and Citizens for Public Justice, joined in this symbolic protest in support of both nature and democracy.[3]

Why are environmental groups so disappointed in Canada's Conservative government?

The reasons are too many to recount in full here. But start with this: on climate issues, the prime minister has publicly questioned the science of climate change, calling it "tentative and contradictory." Famously, he once wrote that "Kyoto is essentially a socialist scheme to suck money out of wealth-producing nations."[4] (By "Kyoto," he was referring to the UN's 1997 global warming protocol.) Canada, under a Liberal government, signed the Kyoto Accord, but successive governments have never met their promised targets. In November 2010, without debate, unelected Conservative senators killed this country's Climate Change Accountability Act, which had been passed in the House of Commons.[5] As the *coup de grâce*, in December 2011 the Conservative government formally withdrew from the Kyoto Accord, making Canada the only country in the world to sign it and then formally withdraw its signature.

More than one-third of the 2012 budget legislation (170-plus pages) dealt with environmental issues. Yet in the Budget Speech itself, there was not a single reference to climate change though there was certainly concern for "the investment climate."[6] This makes plain the government's priorities and its disdain for taking action to address the climate crisis. However, a scientific assessment of Canada's resolve to address global warming was by then on the horizon.

Canada's Climate Record

Scott Vaughan, Canada's Commissioner of the Environment and Sustainable Development, reported to Parliament on May 8, 2012. His report stated that the federal government had not complied with the Kyoto Protocol Implementation Act and that it would not meet its current target for greenhouse gas (GHG) emission reductions of 17 per cent (of the 2005 level) by the year 2020. In fact, Environment Canada's own forecast indicated that by 2020, Canada's emissions would be 7 per cent *above* 2005 levels.

Then on June 13 the National Round Table on the Environment and the Economy (NRTEE) released a report on Canada's GHG commitments. That study tabulated all of the efforts of Canada's provinces as well as the federal government's and found them wanting. This report, titled *Reality Check: The State of Climate Progress in Canada*, is the best analysis of Canadian action to address climate change commitments available to date.

One of that report's key conclusions is that most emission reductions will have to come from the oil and gas sector, followed by manufacturing, electricity generation, and transportation. The same report attempts to price the various costs of meeting Canada's stated targets and concludes that whatever actions are taken, delays will cost us more. The measures that Canada is currently taking will achieve less than half this country's reductions goal. NRTEE argues that Canada needs to put a price on carbon without delay (some provinces have already made tentative steps in this direction; see below).[7]

In response, Bill C-38 took decisive action – but in exactly the *opposite* direction that environmentalists hoped to see. The federal government repealed the Kyoto Protocol Implementation Act and announced that by 2013, it would shut down the National Roundtable on the Economy and the Environment (which is the group that measures Canada's lack of performance on global warming). Bill C-38's passage almost guaranteed that Canada would not meet its GHG reduction commitments.

Can Taxes Help Save the Environment?

Canadians are concerned about their environmental impact. We realize that we must change our wasteful behaviours if we want the earth to continue to provide for us and for future generations. We understand that we must use fewer plastic bags, use less gas in our cars, insulate our homes more carefully, and recycle glass, plastic, and paper.

What in the world does taxation policy have to do with all that?

To change environmentally destructive behaviour, governments must make choices. They can pass legislation to outlaw certain actions, such as adding lead to gasoline. Alternatively, they can regulate certain behaviours – for example, by limiting the volume and toxicity of waste products. However, industry usually opposes restrictions like these, while various publics must be involved in weighing the impacts of regulatory measures. Often, the regulations that are politically palatable either fall short of the best scientific advice or take advantage of weaker regulatory regimes in other jurisdictions (as was the case when Quebec's Liberal government promised subsidies to reopen asbestos mines for export sales).

Another option, one that many societies are now employing, encourages behavioural change by applying market forces and price signals. Sometimes referred to as "eco-taxes," these measures can complement or even avert the need for regulation, while delivering the required results.

"Eco-Taxes"

There are several varieties of "eco-taxes." Some of them are quite familiar to citizens today while others are more avant-garde. For example, paying 5 cents for a plastic bag while shopping has become almost ordinary today. Other familiar "eco-taxes" include camping fees in parks, waste disposal fees, and the purchase of fishing or hunting licences. Some jurisdictions employ car registration taxes (giving cheaper rates to more fuel-efficient models) or tax larger vehicles such as SUVs; the resulting income is then earmarked to subsidize the purchase of hybrid models. Still other countries apply a tax of nearly 100 per cent on cars in order to limit private automobile use. In Germany, eco-taxes are levied on electricity use, though not on power originating from renewable sources. Most often, "eco-taxes" indicate a society's intent to promote a fuller-cost accounting structure in their economies, with greener practices as the overall goal.

To counter negative externalities, societies can "tax the bads," such as water and energy waste, traffic congestion, and urban sprawl. At the same time, they can encourage "positive externalities" by subsidizing public transit, education, and community parks.[8]

The current price structures in our economy actually create environmental problems because they do not price all of the inputs used in production. Today's industrial processes rarely if ever pay for the "dumping" of carbon emissions into the atmosphere, whether that dumping is a by-product of extraction, production, or the transportation of goods to market. One solution is simply to realign incentives (prices) with environmental goals. Society already "taxes the bad, not the good," in order to influence various behaviours – tobacco taxes serve as a disincentive to smoking, for example. Governments also incentivize behaviour that they want to encourage – for example, RRSP deductions are an incentive to save. Taxes and incentives, if well designed, can help bring about change; they can also be more cost-effective and provide broader coverage than regulation.

Tax measures are one not-at-all radical way to achieve ecological justice, especially when the conversation turns to climate change. Options include using currently established taxes, such as fuel taxes, or establishing a new tax, such as a carbon tax. The point in each case is to allow the market to send signals (what economists refer to as "pulling with" as opposed to "against" prices) that will influence behaviour to meet desired societal goals.

An even simpler policy lever, available to Canada right away, would be to eliminate the special tax breaks that the federal government currently extends to companies that produce oil, gas, and coal. Subsidizing the extraction of fossil fuels takes us in the wrong direction – it works against our need to reduce our dependence on artificially low-cost energy sources that add to GHG emissions. By distorting the energy market in this way, Canada is helping companies that are already reaping high profits; it is also making investments in cleaner alternatives like wind and solar power much less attractive. In 2009, at the G20 Summit in Pittsburgh, Canada agreed to phase out more than $1 billion in subsidies and tax breaks to companies producing oil, gas, and coal.[9] Far too tentative steps have been taken to keep that promise. Worse yet, at the Rio+20 conference in June 2012, Canada actually worked to gut a section of the final document that called once again on the international community to end fossil fuel subsidies.[10]

The Case for Pricing Carbon[11]

Tim Flannery reminds us:

> When we consider the fate of the planet as a whole, we must be under no illusions as to what is at stake. Earth's average temperature is around 15 degrees C., and whether we allow it to rise by a single degree, or 3 degrees C., will decide the fate of hundreds of thousands of species, and most probably billions of people.[12]

Many experts agree that putting a price on carbon is one of the most effective ways to reduce GHG emissions, which are the main contributor to climate change.[13] Carbon pricing[14] places a fiscal price, or tax, on the burning of fossil fuels such as heating oil, natural gas, coal, gasoline, and diesel. It requires those who pollute to pay for the environmental damage their activities cause. It internalizes many of the environmental and societal costs related to the production and consumption of carbon-intensive goods and services – costs that current prices often ignore.[15]

Prices in Canada for non-renewable fuels such as gasoline currently do not reflect the environmental damage being done through their production and use. As a result, heavy industries as well as individuals have been slow to employ carbon-reducing measures such as purchasing energy-efficient products, using renewable energy sources (wind, solar, and water power), and practising conservation-based behaviour (such as bicycling, recycling, and using public transit). Carbon pricing, which is fundamentally an economic policy, makes industries and individuals more cognizant of the fossil fuels they use and provides them with a financial incentive to reduce their carbon emissions.[16]

There are two basic approaches to carbon pricing: a carbon tax, and a cap-and-trade system. To administer a carbon tax, the government sets a price per tonne of emissions and adds that cost to the price of the energy source.[17] In B.C., for example, the government has imposed a 6.67¢ per litre carbon tax on gasoline,[18] which gasoline consumers must pay in addition to other taxes.

A cap-and-trade or emissions trading system is a market-based approach to carbon pricing. Under this system the government, or a group of governments, sets a yearly cap or limit on the amount of GHGs that can be emitted by industry. The cap is based on one-tonne "allowances" or "permits," which are distributed or sold to covered industrial sectors. Facilities are not allowed to go over their permitted emission allowances; if they do, they must purchase additional allowances on the market. Facilities that emit less than their permitted allowances may sell their permit surplus on the market or save it for future use. Over time, the number of allowances distributed will decrease, thereby reducing GHG emissions and raising the market value of emission allowances.[19]

Because of the "cap" on GHG emissions, the one distinct environmental advantage that a cap-and-trade system has over a carbon tax is that it provides more certainty about the volume of emission reductions that will be generated. A carbon tax policy, by contrast, requires the government to intervene regularly to ensure that carbon tax levels meet national emission targets. This may become a problem, especially around election time, when politicians are less willing to increase taxes.[20]

Compared to a cap-and-trade system, a carbon tax offers heavy industry and consumers more certainty regarding energy prices. A carbon tax allows governments to lay out a plan prior to implementation, detailing when energy prices will rise and to what extent; this enables industries and individuals to plan for the future with more confidence. Owing to the market-based nature of the cap-and-trade system, energy prices are likely to fluctuate with the whims of the free market (when emission allowances are trading at a high price, energy prices soar; when allowances are trading at a reduced price, energy prices plummet).[21] Proponents of a carbon tax also point out that it can be implemented quite easily and quickly using many of the administrative structures already built into the tax system. Conversely, a cap-and-trade system requires the establishment of an emissions trading market, with subsequent operational guidelines, all of which take time to develop.[22]

The Planet Burns, the Provinces Act – While Ottawa Fiddles

In Canada, Quebec and B.C. have already implemented a carbon tax as a way to reduce GHG emissions.

On October 1, 2007, Quebec became the first province in Canada to institute a carbon tax. Quebec is committed to reducing its GHG emissions by 20 per cent by 2020 (based on 1990 levels); its target, then, is comparable to that of the European Union and also outpaces Ottawa's targets. If it achieves its goal, Quebec will have North America's lowest emissions rate per capita, making it a key player in the battle against climate change.[23]

Quebec's carbon tax covers emissions from oil, natural gas, and coal. It requires oil producers to pay an additional 0.8¢ per litre for gasoline and 0.9¢ per litre for diesel fuel. Though these are relatively mild tax rates, at the time that Quebec introduced its carbon tax, estimates were that it would cost producers $69 million annually for gasoline, $36 million for diesel fuel, and $43 million for heating oil. Natural gas distributors were expected to pay $39 million annually.[24] In 2013, Quebec will be changing to a cap-and-trade system, with 2012 as a transition year.[25]

On July 1, 2008, B.C. joined Quebec in instituting a carbon tax. This one covers around 70 per cent of GHG emissions.[26] The government phased in the tax over four years, based on an initial $10 per tonne for carbon emissions with annual increases of $5 per tonne. On July 1, 2012, the last year of the phase-in, the carbon tax rose to $30 per tonne.[27] Like Quebec, B.C. has set its carbon tax rates relative to the amount of carbon found in each of the taxable fossil fuels; thus, jet fuel is taxed more heavily than propane.[28] The B.C. government estimates that its carbon tax will generate $1.85 billion in revenues by 2012, with all of that money being recycled back into the economy through tax credits and reduced personal and corporate tax rates.[29]

Besides implementing a carbon tax, B.C. and Quebec belong to the Western Climate Initiative (WCI), a partnership that is seeking to reduce GHG emissions through a multi-regional cap-and-trade system. Other participants in WCI include Ontario, Manitoba, Arizona, Washington, Oregon, California, Montana, Utah, and New Mexico.[30] By 2015, when the program is set to be fully implemented, more than 90 per cent of GHG emissions[31] will be covered by the cap-and-trade system. Emission sources covered include the following: electricity generation (including electricity imported by WCI members), industrial fuel combustion, industrial processes, transportation fuel use, and residential and commercial fuel use. WCI's first phase was launched on January 1, 2012, and covers electricity (and electricity imports), industrial combustion at large sources, and industrial process emissions for which sufficient measurement methods exist. The program's goal is to reduce GHG emissions by 15 per cent below 2005 levels by 2020.[32]

The European Union's twenty-seven member-states, along with Iceland, Liechtenstein, and Norway, have set up their own Emissions Trading System (EU ETS) based on the cap-and-trade principle. The EU's program covers carbon dioxide emissions from power stations, combustion plants, oil refineries, and steel works, as well as factories that produce cement, glass, lime, bricks, ceramics, pulp, paper, and board. Nitrous oxide emissions are sometimes also covered.[33] Starting in 2012, the EU ETS will also cover emissions from all domestic and international flights that arrive at or depart from EU airports.[34] The goal of the EU ETS is to reduce GHG emissions by 21 per cent below 2005 levels by 2020.[35]

On July 1, 2012, Australia introduced a price for each tonne of CO2 emissions, at $23. This will rise (in real terms) to $24.15 in 2013 and to $25.40 in 2014.[36]

Carbon Pricing – a Helpful Way Forward?

The UN's Intergovernmental Panel on Climate Change, the world's premier climate science body, has stated that if the dangerous consequences of climate change are to be avoided, the earth's atmospheric temperature cannot rise more than 2°C above pre-industrial levels. To achieve this goal, industrialized nations must commit to reducing their combined GHG emissions by 25 to 40 per cent below 1990 levels by 2020.[37] Dr. Marc Jaccard, Canada's foremost climate change economist, has shown that in order to reach the 2°C target, Canada must impose a $50 per tonne carbon price immediately, increasing it to $200 per tonne by 2020.[38]

The most authoritative report on the economic implications of global climate change was produced in October 2006 by Sir Nicholas Stern. His 700-page review states that climate change is the greatest and widest-ranging market failure ever seen and that by 2050, climate change could impose costs equalling 20 per cent of the global GDP. However, "strong early action" costing 1 per cent of annual global GDP could minimize damage. Stern's three main recommendations focus on carbon pricing, technology policy, and the removal of barriers to behavioural change.[39]

The UN has concluded that a tax on carbon dioxide emissions in developed countries of $25 per tonne would raise around $250 billion per year. This money could be used, it continues, to counter the implications of climate change and underdevelopment in the global South at a time when many donor nations (including Canada) have cut their overseas development assistance budgets.[40]

Many other experts have agreed that to reduce carbon emissions, it will be necessary to put a price on carbon, whether that entails a carbon tax or a cap-and-trade system. It is also clear that in Canada, political will for such policies is lacking – the governing Conservative Party has an ideological aversion to increasing *any* kind of tax.

Also in Canada, the New Democrats, Liberals, and Bloc Québécois all openly support cap-and-trade schemes to reduce carbon emissions. Only the Green Party supports a carbon tax instead, which would include a "carbon tariff" on fossil fuel exports to countries that do not have a carbon tax themselves.[41]

The Conservative government has described its strategy for reducing GHG emissions as a "sector by sector" approach based on regulating high-emitting sectors of the economy. It has developed vehicle emission regulations to ensure that vehicles on Canadian roads meet U.S. standards. As well, and importantly, Ottawa plans to implement regulations on coal-fired generating plants.

The National Round Table on the Environment and the Economy contends that Ottawa's proposals so far are timid ones that will result in Canada reaching about one-half of its emissions target. The government rails against carbon taxes, yet its plans to regulate generating stations are essentially taxes. The outgoing president of NRTEE, David McLaughlin, has noted that "when the government regulates environmental outcomes, as they're doing with their 'sector-by-sector' approach, that imposes costs. It's called shadow pricing, and that too is a form of carbon pricing."[42]

Some organizations, such as the Green Budget Coalition,[43] have attempted to engage governments by talking about "environmental fiscal reform," rather than "taxes" – a hot-button word that some politicians feel enshrines less-than-noble intentions.

The Need for Action

Some of those involved in the recent international negotiations on GHG emissions feel that new strategies will be necessary in the wake of the failed UN conferences at Copenhagen and Durban. Stéphane Dion, Canada's former Liberal leader and a proponent of the "Green Shift," has proposed that international efforts be refocused on negotiating a "global carbon price signal." This would be "harmonized in principle but flexible in practice" and would provide better results than the current practice of attempting to convince countries to accept stricter national targets for quantitative reductions in GHG emissions.[44]

Other efforts focus on pushing Canada to lead on the GHG file. These have been encouraged by provincial actions that can complement emissions reductions. For example, in the 2012 Alternative Federal Budget (AFB), prepared by a wide range of Canadian civil society organizations and academics, a national Harmonized Carbon Tax (HCT) was proposed. AFB economists maintain that such a tax, if set at $30 per tonne commencing on July 1, 2013, could generate more than $14 billion in fiscal year 2013–14, rising to more than $17 billion in 2014–15.[45]

And such proposals are not limited to opposition politicians, academics, and environmental activists. Lorraine Mitchelmore, President of Shell Canada and a member of the Canadian Council of Chief Executives, acknowledges that Canada is one of the world's highest per capita GHG emitters and has called for a carbon pricing mechanism.[46] Researchers at the Sustainable Prosperity think tank are calling for "pollution taxes" as a substitute for income taxes; this approach would decouple overall tax revenues from labour income (something that is important in view of Canada's aging population and that could better maintain Canada's capacity to provide necessary services to seniors).[47]

All taxation and subsidy measures must, of course, be fair and be seen as fair. Environmental taxes can be regressive, with a disproportionate impact on those with low and middle incomes. Regressive taxes, by definition, increase inequality, and user fees are one form of them. But "green" taxes are not inherently progressive or regressive – it all depends on how they are designed.

If the public is to support green taxes, such as a carbon tax, they must perceive those taxes as both smart and fair – as taxing pollution (a "bad"), not jobs (a "good"). These taxes can be designed to support the "green-collar economy"[48] and to create jobs that support the triple-dividend of social, economic, and environmental progress. And since the tax system itself can be used to redistribute wealth and close the growing gap between the rich and poor in Canada, carbon tax measures should be designed to reduce income inequality.

The richest 20 per cent of Canadians generate 1.8 times more GHGs per capita than the poorest 20 per cent. So it would seem logical to organize measures to ensure that those who emit more pay more than those who emit less.[49]

"It is important to develop an approach to reduce emissions that does not have an unequal impact on families with lower incomes, who have lower emissions to begin with," says Marc Lee. "Those with higher incomes are able to reduce their emissions – by reducing air travel and investing in home energy efficiency – more easily than low-income families, without affecting their basic needs."

There is no question that Canada must put a price on carbon. The money raised from a carbon tax or a cap-and-trade system should go to low income credits and for programs that help families and businesses to adapt their practices and their homes and buildings and encourage the development of new, green practices and technologies. In this way, income from carbon taxes would decrease inequality as well as improve the environment.

8

Tax Justice and the Civil Economy

JOHN RESTAKIS

It has been a long time since the question of fairness has played so prominent a role in Canadian politics. Issues of class, social and economic inequity, and the state's role in representing the public interest are now taking centre stage as the Harper administration attempts to consolidate the primacy of capital and corporate interests through a wholesale remaking of the Canadian body politic. The government's approach to this involves four aggressive lines of action: dismantling Ottawa's capacity to check corporate interests, particularly with respect to the environment; destroying independent sources of knowledge and information; terminating and discrediting state support for social programs and the social economy; and silencing the opposition.

We have entered the era of the petro-state in Canada. Rarely before have the interests of government and of capital corresponded so closely in this country. The speed of these changes has left many Canadians in shock. The changes are deep, pervasive, and – most disturbing of all – so sweeping that any hope of re-establishing what took generations to build will bear what are clearly intended to be insupportable costs. Unless they find the monumental political will and the bold vision to remobilize capital to rebuild and defend the public interest, Canadians will have lost a priceless social patrimony.

In the current political environment, tax policy has moved to the heart of social and economic justice debates in Canada. And not only in Canada. In the United States in 2012, income inequality emerged as the defining issue in the most polarized political climate in living memory. Meanwhile in Europe, the shock doctrine of austerity is destroying the social safety net in one country after another and the sins of the privileged are being ransomed by the sacrifices of everyone else.

Everyone finally understands that questions of fairness, of social justice, of who is entitled to what from our economic system lie at the heart of what shapes Canada, the United States, and the larger global economy. Everything is at stake, since to address inequality is to confront the one question that defines our economic system and its underlying ideology as well as the politics that perpetuate it.

This is the background against which discussions of tax justice take place. To ignore the tax system, or to constrain questions about fair taxation to particular policies or systems without addressing deeper issues of systemic inequity, is to cede victory to those forces that are perpetuating that inequity. Sustained attacks on tax fairness are playing a central role in the ongoing assault on political and economic equality. Tax policy today is a potent reminder that global society is being shaped by warring values and world views.

The discussion that follows is framed around two basic ideas. The first is that any discussion of tax justice must start from the premise that taxation is a social good. Questions of tax justice and legitimacy are, at their root, social and moral. Otherwise, those questions would have little meaning – whether applied to tax systems as a whole or to individual taxation policies. To concede that justice should be an attribute of tax policy is to acknowledge a moral basis for taxation. The question, then, is not "Should a tax system be just?", but rather, "What is just, and how does tax policy promote or undermine justice?"

The second point is that the fairness of a tax system cannot be isolated from the fairness of the economic system in which it operates. An unfair economic system (i.e., one that is based on exploiting the majority for the benefit of the few) will always produce tax policies that reflect and reinforce that underlying unfairness. The broader question, then, is "How might a tax system help redress the institutional injustice of the economic system itself?" Tax policy is never only about taxes. It is always ultimately about politics.

For these reasons, I approach the question of tax justice from the standpoint of economic democracy and the use of market forces to pursue social ends. Here again, I focus on two questions: How does tax policy promote the expansion of democracy in the economy, particularly through the use of co-op models? And how does tax policy catalyze the expansion and maturation of the broader civil or social economy?

The question of the social economy is central, for it is key to developing a new approach to understanding how the public interest is understood and upheld. The economic activity generated by the social economy in the Western democracies is huge – and growing. As a percentage of the total economy, for example, Canada's non-profit workforce is the world's second largest. With an estimated economic turnover of $75.8 billion, Canadian non-profits account for 8.5 per cent of the country's GDP (when the economic value of volunteer efforts is included). Canadian non-profits account for around 2.1 million full-time-equivalent employees, nearly matching the 2.3 million employees reported by Canada's manufacturing sector.[1] If we include the economic worth of co-ops, credit unions, and social enterprises, the economic value of the non-profit sector is far higher.

I begin with the case of co-operatives because they are an instructive example of how tax policy intersects with political, economic, and social issues in the broader context of fairness.

Taxation and the Co-op Model

Co-ops are unique in that they serve both social and commercial purposes. Co-ops can be commercial, for-profit entities or they can devote themselves mainly to social and non-profit aims. In either case, they are different from both capitalist enterprises and conventional non-profit societies in that they are owned collectively and have a democratic structure, one that confers equal rights on all members regardless of their capital investment. Most important, co-ops are driven equally by social and economic ends. In this, they are unlike capitalist firms, whose primary purpose is to maximize profits for investors.

The importance placed on the social bonds of membership is what defines co-ops primarily as associations of people with a mutual purpose (as opposed to mere collections of capital). Co-ops mobilize capital in the service of social ends, whether those ends are defined as the collective aims of the membership or – as in the case of social or community service co-ops – the production of goods and services for a broader community purpose (health care, affordable housing, recreational services, etc.). And whereas a capitalist firm may allocate a portion of its commercial profits to charitable donations, community events, and other social ends, such ends are always subordinate to the profit motive. If a company were to terminate its corporate social aims, this would not in the least affect its primary character or purpose. If a co-op were to do so, it would cease, for all intents and purposes, to be a co-op.

The tax treatment of co-ops differs from that of conventional capitalist enterprises largely as a function of the *purposes* to which capital is put. And as I will argue shortly, these same purposes constitute the basis for an entirely different taxation approach to organizations that collectively constitute what we call the social economy. What all these organizations have in common, regardless of whether they seek to generate profits, is that they utilize capital to realize social benefits.

Though they are distinct in their purpose and structure, co-operatives in Canada and abroad have generally been afforded few tax breaks. With a few exceptions, co-ops are generally treated as profit-earning enterprises, with little consideration given to the social purposes to which their capital is put. Only when co-ops are structured as non-profits are their social dimensions recognized for tax purposes. In jurisdictions that recognize non-profit co-ops (such as community service co-ops in BC, and solidarity co-ops in Quebec), they are subject to the same controls as apply to other non-profits.

As with the tax treatment of non-profits, the refusal to recognize that co-ops are unique in both nature and purpose reflects a distorted view of enterprises, markets, and the operations of the economy as a whole. It will come as no surprise that in all but a handful of jurisdictions, the tax treatment of co-ops reflects a political and institutional bias that promotes the primacy of capitalist firms. Tax systems in the West uphold a neoliberal conception of the free market as the standard against which all enterprises and economic practices are to be measured.

Typically, the only area in which co-ops receive special consideration relates to the treatment of patronage refunds to members. Patronage refunds are provided to members on the basis of how much business they do with the co-op. This is among the very oldest co-op practices, having been established early on as a means to repay members' loyalty by offering discounts on goods purchased. It has been a staple of co-op practice since the 1800s. At a time when access to capital was among the chief obstacles to the operation of co-ops – an obstacle that remains to this day – a second distinctive feature of co-ops was that they issued equity interest instead of cash as a form of patronage payment. In either case, patronage refunds, whether they take the form of a cash refund or an equity share, are considered the property and income of the member, not the co-op; thus, they are taxable income to the member rather than to the co-op. The tax exemption is based solely on an interpretation of who owns the patronage dividend rather than on the purposes to which the co-op's surplus is applied.

Questions of purpose, however, should be fundamental to any consideration of how a tax system treats the income of an enterprise. And it is precisely in those jurisdictions that recognize the broader social benefits provided by co-operatives that these organizations enjoy distinctive treatment that extends beyond narrow questions of personal income.

Three cases in particular are instructive: Italy, where co-ops are protected by the constitution; Spain, where the Mondragon co-ops are universally recognized for their economic and social benefits; and Quebec, which has the largest and most advanced co-op sector in North America.

Co-ops represent an approach to tax policy that rewards social forms of capital, which by definition are distinct from both private capital and conventional non-profits. They are a good starting point for exploring the broader ramifications of tax policy not only for the social economy but also for civil society, and for considering as well the growing contradiction between prevailing public policy and the public good.

Italy

Italy has the highest concentration of co-ops in the Western world. There are more than 70,000 co-ops in Italy, 16,000 of which are producer co-ops. With more than 5 million members, Italy's consumer co-op movement is second in size only to Japan's, and the country's social co-ops now account for over 60 per cent of Italy's home and health care services. Indeed, Italian co-ops are today among the largest and most successful of Italy's firms. Over the past twenty years, the Italian corporate sector has been cutting its workforce, but the largest of Italy's co-ops have been growing in both size and reach and outpacing their competitors both in the number of jobs they are creating and in market share.[2] In the retail sector, Italy's co-op system has enjoyed nearly 15 per cent growth while keeping prices 5 per cent lower than most supermarkets and 2 to 3 per cent lower than those of their fiercest competitors.[3]

Despite the remarkable commercial success of Italy's co-ops, the country's tax regime recognizes and promotes them as a form of enterprise that *socializes markets*. And as stated by Flavio del Bono, the former finance minister of Emilia-Romagna,[4] the massive presence of co-ops is not only a stabilizing factor in the regional economy, protecting jobs and promoting economic development, but also a key factor in the region's economic equity. Besides being an economic leader in Italy, the region enjoys the country's lowest levels of income disparity and the highest percentage of women in the workforce. This has been made possible by the region's active support of home and child care support for families. Protecting this social purpose of co-ops is an explicit aim of Italy's tax law.

Italy has developed a number of innovative and preferential taxation mechanisms for co-ops. A key support has been the Basevi Law, enacted in 1947, which provides co-ops with a tax exemption on their indivisible reserves in order to encourage self-capitalization.[5] Considering that Italy's current corporate income tax rate for privately owned businesses is 31.4 per cent, this exemption is significant. In 2003, the exemption was reduced from 100 per cent to 70 per cent for co-ops that were doing more than half their business with members and to 30 per cent for those that were doing less.[6]

Indivisible reserves are capital pools that belong to the co-op as a whole and may not be distributed to individual members. Under Italian law, every co-op must place some of its surplus in this reserve. The indivisible reserve is viewed as a social asset to be used for the sustenance of the co-op and to generate employment and wealth creation for the community as a whole, not just existing co-op members. This asset is passed on as a patrimony from one generation of co-op members to the next. In its purest sense, it is a form of social capital generated by the logic of collective ownership,[7] and Italians justify the tax exemption for co-ops on the basis of their social function. If a co-op dissolves, the reserve goes to a charity. The concept of indivisible reserves will have important implications for our later discussion of a new role for non-profits and other social purpose organizations.

In 1985 the Italian government passed the Marcora Act, which further encouraged the establishment of worker-owned co-ops as job creators. This Act created a fund to assist the development of new co-ops, especially those created by workers facing job loss as a result of business bankruptcies, business sales and relocations, owner retirement, or other reasons.[8]

In 1992, Law No. 59 required that co-ops contribute 3 per cent of their surplus to mutual funds managed by the co-op federation to which they belonged. The purpose of these funds is to support the start-up and development of new co-ops and the expansion of existing ones. Like contributions to indivisible reserves, these contributions are tax-exempt. Today, these funds are a major source of the capital behind co-op growth and innovation.

Social Co-ops and Social Welfare

In 1991, Italy passed Law No. 381, which established the foundations for social co-ops as a means to create a wide range of social services for Italians. But unlike conventional co-ops, whose purpose is mainly to provide services to their own members, the law stipulates that social co-ops must have as their purpose "to pursue the general community interest in promoting human concerns and the integration of citizens." Social co-ops are recognized as having goals that promote benefits to the community and its citizens, not solely to co-op members. Moreover, Italian legislation acknowledges the affinity between public bodies and social co-ops in the promotion of public welfare, emphasizing the desirability of collaboration between them. For this reason, many social co-ops receive public funding in the form of operating subsidies that offset labour costs. They also enjoy greater flexibility than other forms of enterprise with regard to labour legislation.

Social co-ops that draw at least 30 per cent of their employees from marginalized and disadvantaged groups – which include the handicapped, the elderly, youth, people with intellectual impairments, and excluded groups such as ex-prisoners, minors at risk, and drug addicts – are exempted from paying payroll costs. The state picks up those costs as an incentive for co-ops to hire people who face employment barriers.

A further development in the treatment of social co-ops has to do with membership. Italian law provides that the ownership structure of social co-ops may be comprised of several categories of members (workers, users, volunteers, investors, and public bodies), all of which have an interest in the services being provided. This multi-stakeholder aspect has done much to allow social co-ops to pursue more public aims. It also reflects the expanding focus on community service as opposed to the traditional co-op focus on benefiting members. Compared to traditional non-profits, these new organizations rely far more on the broader representation of stakeholder interests and on participative and democratic management than they do on the traditional constraints on profit distribution.

The experience of social co-ops in Italy has led to a radical rethinking of how the public interest might best be served by entities other than the state. Today, social co-ops account for roughly 20 per cent of Italy's spending on social services. In the city of Bologna, over 87 per cent of social care services are delivered through service agreements with social co-ops.

For many decades, the tax treatment of co-ops in Italy represented an unusually enlightened policy with respect to recognizing the social benefits implicit in co-op enterprises. That treatment was also the product of a particular political philosophy deeply influenced by co-operative and socialist principles. All of this started to change, however, when Silvio Berlusconi was elected President of Italy in 2003. Recognizing that the co-op movement was a bastion of resistance to his policies, Berlusconi, with the support of Italy's corporate sector, attempted to break the power of the co-ops by attacking the tax exemptions as they applied to the corporate income tax and to indivisible reserves. The result was a mass uprising in 2005, during which more than a million people converged on Rome to protest the changes. It was the largest mass gathering in Italy since the end of the Second World War.

In the end, a compromise was reached. Indivisible reserves would be subject to taxation if more than 50 per cent of a co-op's business was with non-members. The principle that capital with a social purpose should be treated differently from private capital was, however, never questioned.

Spain

As in Italy, co-ops in Spain receive a substantial corporate tax advantage compared to privately owned firms. The corporate income tax rate for co-ops is 10 per cent of profit compared to 28 per cent for private corporations. This represents a major benefit and a key policy that has enabled Spain's co-op sector to achieve the strength, capacity, and autonomy it enjoys today. In Spain's Basque region, the Mondragon co-ops have created a dense network of sophisticated institutions and services, including a social security system, financial institutions such as the Caja Laboral co-operative bank, training and research centres, and Mondragon University, among others.

Taken together, this system is one of the world's most successful co-op economies and leads Spain in the production of manufactured products and their export to the global market. Moreover, while the global economic recession has flatlined economic growth in Spain, the Mondragon co-ops continue to support the local economy, which has the lowest unemployment in the country. And while overdependence on tourism, finance, and property speculation has weakened the Spanish economy, the Mondragon co-ops have continued to focus on research, innovation, and manufacturing and continue to export. The region has the highest per capita output in Spain – €31,288 compared to a national average of €23,271 and an EU average of €25,134.[9] This is an astonishing testament to the durability of co-op enterprises during hard times. And, like the co-ops of Emilia-Romagna, Mondragon's co-ops have attained a global scale and reach.

The cultivation of co-operative social values is woven into the country's tax code. Spanish law requires that each co-op establish a social fund, to which it must allocate 10 per cent of its surplus. The law also stipulates how the funds may be used – for example, to train the co-op's members, managers, and board directors and to foster community and environmental initiatives.[10]

Another Spanish law, similar to the Italian one, promotes the long-term stability and financial strength of co-operative assets by requiring each co-op to place 20 per cent of its annual net surplus in an indivisible reserve. This reserve is also supported by contributions from individual members. When joining a co-op, the new member must contribute a "threshold payment," which is deposited in an individualized capital account (ICA). That account is adjusted upwards for inflation each year, and its value increases by an interest rate of about 6 per cent.[11] Of this threshold payment, 15 to 25 per cent is a nonrefundable contribution to the co-op's indivisible reserve. For new members who cannot afford the cost up front, the payment can be made through salary deductions over a three-year period.[12] As well as being invested in the co-op's reserve, a significant portion of the co-op's net surplus each year is allocated to the members' ICA accounts in proportion to each member's hours of work. The ICA remains in the co-op until the member retires or leaves the business.

This system of member equity contribution, which is similar to that used by many worker co-ops in Italy, not only ensures a substantial and autonomous source of working capital for the co-op but also amounts to a de facto retirement plan for members once they leave. This is one reason why Spain's co-ops are a powerful source of social welfare, and it is easy to see why the state recognizes and treats co-operatives as social assets. Tax support for indivisible reserves helps secure the co-ops' long-term future and maintain the employment and broader economic benefits they offer to Spanish citizens. This collective social benefit is both recognized and rewarded.

This combination of lower taxes, reserves, and ICAs means that Spain's co-ops retain 80 per cent of their annual surpluses as ongoing assets. This significantly enhances their strength and viability compared to other corporate models.[13]

Quebec

Over the past twenty years, Quebec has far outpaced the rest of Canada in the strength, diversity, and dynamism of new co-op development. This impressive growth is due in part to legislative changes that have created two new variations on the traditional co-op model: the solidarity co-op, and the worker–shareholder co-op.[14] Solidarity co-ops, which are based on the social co-ops of Italy, follow a multi-stakeholder model that allows three types of members in one co-operative: consumers, workers, and solidarity members (usually local organizations).

The worker–shareholder co-op model allows workers to use a co-op to collectively purchase shares in the company they work for. In this way, workers acquire stock voting rights according to the co-op's share of ownership. The co-op's votes in the private company are determined by the number of participating workers and based on a one-member, one-vote formula.[15] The co-op acquires a portion of the company's profits and takes part in its decision making. Besides benefiting the workers, this model enables the company to acquire expansion capital, to promote innovation and efficiency, and to enhance the loyalty and performance of its workers.

In 1985 the Quebec government established the Régime d'investissement coopératif (Co-operative Investment Tax Incentive), which supports the growth of co-ops by extending to members and workers a personal income tax deduction of up to 150 per cent of any capital invested in the co-op. It also created Investment Quebec, a government corporation that established a $140 million fund to provide loans to co-ops.

The Quebec government has also supported co-ops by investing in Regional Development Co-operatives (RDCs). RDCs are local networks of co-ops and credit unions that work directly on co-op development projects. Their funding formula is based on the number of jobs created or saved through the co-op program. Since they were founded, RDCs have been stronger employment generators than either government or private firms. This, coupled with the survival rate of co-ops – nearly double that of private firms[16] – is another reason why the province continues to support the sector.

But another reason for this support has to do with the growing influence of the province's social economy. The extension of social capital philosophy embodied in co-ops to the social economy as a whole has the potential to radically alter power relations between the state, the private sector, and the social economy itself.

Tax Policy and the Social Economy

A great deal has been written recently on the subject of the social economy. Over the past decade in particular, this interest among academics and policy makers has coincided with the acceleration of two trends: growing criticisms levelled against conventional free market theories of economics, and the retreat of governments from their role as providers of public goods. These two factors have thrown a spotlight on the operations and potential of a sector that until now has been consigned to the shadows of economic thinking. The recent "discovery" of the social economy has been a feature of the broader rediscovery of civil society itself, which began with the collapse of the Soviet model and with efforts to salvage from that wreckage a progressive conception of society and economics – one that relies neither on the failed dogmas of state socialism associated with the Soviet Bloc, nor on the neoliberal dogmas promoted by free marketeers.

The recent resurrection of the civil society tradition has recast the political and economic debate within a political economy frame that had been abandoned in the early 1900s. Inconvenient questions of fairness, of political and economic justice, and of social good versus neoliberal economism have returned with a vengeance as our economic system further erodes the notion that economics, as a body of theory and practice, serves the public interest.

Social Economy and the Public Good

In its broadest sense, civil society develops from the social impulse to engage in free and democratic association, to create community, and to perfect the operations of social life, including its politics. This is the view of civil society that has been adopted by thinkers such as Vaclav Havel.[17] Modern conceptions of civil society distinguish it from the state and from the operations of the private sector. Some writers also distinguish it from the family.

For Havel and a long line of thinkers extending back to Aristotle, civil society is the elementary fact of human existence. It is what makes human life possible. Aristotle believed that civil society was both the means and the end of human association and that the good life was in essence a *social* life. In this sense, the institutions that arise from civil society (schools, voluntary associations, trade unions, courts, political parties, etc.) are what provide individuals with the means to realize their own humanity and by so doing to perfect the whole of society. The state is an outgrowth of this impulse.

Within civil society, a huge portion of civic activities are carried out by organizations created to provide goods and services through collaboration – that is, by people acting together to realize mutual aims. These organizations include non-profit and voluntary groups, service groups, cultural organizations, charities, trade unions, and co-operatives. This economic aspect of civil society is sometimes referred to as the *third sector* or the *social economy*.

And while there is a growing body of research that seeks to measure the size and economic value of the social economy, almost all of this measuring is based on principles and concepts derived from the capitalist economy – that is, the valuing of goods and services based on the exchange values that characterize commercial transactions in the private sector. These values are based on the concept of the exchange of equivalents.

Put simply, the exchange of equivalents means the exchange of one thing for another on the basis of an agreed-upon value. But while this is appropriate for measuring commercial exchange, the determination of value solely on the basis of commercial principles is wholly inadequate for describing the character and needs of the social economy. This is because the social economy is not primarily about exchanging things of equivalent monetary value in pursuit of private ends; rather, it is about creating and utilizing social relations for the pursuit of social ends. A market for things is clearly not the same as a market for social ends.

Attempts to measure value and to develop social and economic policies for the social economy solely on the basis of commercial principles marginalize and misrepresent the social economy even further. As in the case of co-ops, the justification for extending tax supports to social economy organizations such as non-profits and charities is that they generate social benefits that are worth supporting because they are in the public interest. In Canada and across the industrialized West, the principle of tax exemptions for non-profits is well established, for it reflects commonly held attitudes toward charitable giving.

As far back as the Middle Ages, charitable organizations – associated primarily with the church – were exempted from paying income tax, as were churches. These organizations were viewed as taking up a burden that would otherwise have been borne by the state – a burden that included providing poor relief, running hospitals, and caring for widows and orphans. In return for these services, the state compensated organizations through tax exemptions. But it was a condition of these exemptions that these organizations could not retain their profits or distribute them to their governors or members. This legal constraint on profit distribution continues to define non-profits.

But in an age in which social economy organizations are far more complex and sophisticated than simple charity models, and in which hybrid models such as social enterprises and community benefit companies employ market mechanisms to pursue social goals, the old tax exemptions based on constraints to the distribution of profit are wholly inadequate. They fail to capture both the reality and the potential of the social economy as a sector deserving treatment that is equal, on its own terms, to that granted the private and public sectors. They also perpetuate the false notion that profit generation is incompatible with the pursuit of social benefits. This is because profit is still conceived strictly in capitalist terms, which is to say as a private good. But what about profit that is a social good, a collective asset, as in the case of co-ops? The real matter at hand is not profit but rather the purposes for which that profit is created and utilized. Recognition that profit is a social asset has game-changing implications, not only for the social economy but also for how the public interest is defined, developed, and defended.

What we need are social and economic policies, and tax structures as well, that recognize the social and mutual foundations of the social economy as a distinct sphere with its own requirements. On what basis could such policies, and such markets, operate? The answer is found in the economic principle at the heart of social economy organizations and of the social economy as a whole – reciprocity.

On Reciprocity

For both civil society and the social economy, the notion of reciprocity is fundamental. Reciprocity is the social mechanism that makes associational life possible. It is the foundation of social life and of social capital – the predisposition of people in a society to work together towards mutual goals. Reciprocity is a system of voluntary exchange among individuals based on the understanding that the giving of a favour by an individual will later be reciprocated either to the giver or to someone else.

It is instructive to consider how reciprocity relates to the logic and purpose of taxation. If taxation is primarily a means to extract money from a population in order to benefit an elite (whether a monarch or an aristocracy or our own 1 per cent), then there is no reciprocity; what we have instead is a system of legitimized looting. But if taxation is a means whereby everyone contributes a fair portion, the result of which will be the sharing of public goods that benefit everyone, then reciprocity is a defining attribute.

There is a correlation between reciprocity and tax fairness. In the same vein, a tax system's character is an important index of a society's character. Do people pay their taxes, or do they cheat? Do people think of taxes as a public good or as a private burden? The answers to these questions are related to the degree to which taxes embody the principle of reciprocity, and also to the strength of social capital in a community. High levels of social capital – of generalized trust – prompt people to pay their taxes because they believe that others are paying their taxes as well. The opposite is true in societies with low levels of generalized trust: people avoid paying taxes if they feel either that the tax system is unfair or that others are not paying their share. Comparisons of tax systems thus go a long way towards illuminating not only essential differences between one society and another but also what shifts in tax policy tell us about a given society over time.

How governments tax their citizens has a profound impact not only on the state's capacity to promote the common good but also on the public attitudes on which healthy and cohesive communities are based. What, then, does it say about Canada that our current leaders – supported by increasing numbers of Canadians – are calling for as little taxation as possible? And that taxes are increasingly seen as a burden rather than a duty? And that more and more of the tax burden is being shifted away from the wealthy and towards those less able to pay? The answer is not comforting: these things are eroding the shared values that underpin the social contract between government and citizenry and they are reducing support for and recognition of the public good. A glance south of our border, where the very idea of the public good is collapsing, indicates where this leads.

Reciprocity animates a vast range of economic activities that rely on shared values and the connections between people. The social bonds that connect the individual to the human community are based on it. In reciprocal transactions between individuals, it is not simply particular goods, services, and favours that are being exchanged; more fundamentally, these exchanges are expressions of goodwill and the assurance that one is prepared to help others. Reciprocity is the foundation of trust. It is also society's means to build up its stock of social capital. Clearly, then, the practice of reciprocity has profound social and moral implications. It follows that societies are profoundly affected by the degree to which tax systems embody and reinforce this value.

Reciprocity is a key for understanding how society's institutions work; it is also an economic principle with distinct characteristics that embody social as opposed to merely commercial attributes. When reciprocity finds economic expression in the exchange of goods and services among people and communities, a social economy results. Examples range from the provision of burial services through the creation of friendly societies in the 1800s to the promotion of safety through organizations like Neighbourhood Watch today.

Finally, in the moment it is exercised, reciprocity is egalitarian – it presupposes a direct relationship of equality between the individuals involved. It is very different from altruism, where the giver may have no relation to the receiver and where there is a clear asymmetry of power, as is the case with charity.

Social economy organizations, like their co-operative antecedents, pursue their goals, be they economic or social, on the basis that individuals' contributions will be reciprocated and that the benefits will be shared. Reciprocity is the economic principle that defines both the activities and the aims of these organizations, whether they are co-operatives, volunteer organizations, or conventional non-profits. Their primary purpose is to promote collective benefit. Their products are not just the particular goods or services they produce, but human solidarity and social capital. And, in contrast to the capitalist principle that capital controls labour, reciprocity is the means by which social interests – whether these take the form of labour, or citizen groups, or consumers – can exercise control over capital. As a sub-division of civil society, reciprocity for economic purposes is what distinguishes the social economy from the private and public sectors.

There are, of course, many ways in which tax policy can support the development of social economy organizations that provide collective benefits, using the same rationale as that used to support co-operatives in the examples cited above. The first is to extend tax exemptions and benefits to investments in social economy organizations. These are already provided to groups that have acquired charitable status. But there is a compelling case for extending these exemptions for contributions made by supporters – whether association members or other community supporters – to any organization whose primary purpose is the provision of a social good.

Conventional non-profits and a wide range of social enterprises should be able to generate capital for their services through tax-exempt contributions sourced from within civil society itself. The dependence of social economy organizations on the state would thereby be mitigated, and the perennial rationing of capital arising from the social economy's dependence on state funding would be lessened. But for this to happen, the notion that non-profits' goals are incompatible with the generation and utilization of capital (profit) has to be left behind. That notion is a relic of a false understanding: that profit is only a private good and that markets are exclusively capitalist.

A social economy understanding of markets, and of profits (in the case of co-operatives), makes it possible to rethink social legislation in such a manner as to allow non-profits to issue shares to raise capital, to accumulate capital in the form of undistributed reserves for the pursuit of social goods, and to invest in other social economy organizations and institutions that have the same purpose. The development of the kinds of social purpose capital that are now possible in the case of co-operatives should be extended to the whole of the social economy, with the proviso that their use be transparent and democratically accountable to contributors and service users.

This is essential. Without such accountability, there is the risk that the capital accumulated by an organization for social purposes will ultimately be used to pursue private interests, as is the case with some non-profits today that have no structure for accountability to stakeholders. To protect the pursuit of social ends, it is not necessary to prohibit the accumulation and distribution of profit; rather, social constraints must be imposed through democratic accountability for the use of that capital. Exactly the same principle protects the public interest when applied to the state's taxing and spending practices.

Renewed interest in civil society and the social economy is challenging the old market paradigm of society as composed of two sectors – the private and the public. But from the start, the notion of civil economy (as it was then called) was a reaction against the narrow reading of economics as a specialized field of practice divorced from society. This is the larger frame in which the social economy has its original meaning. Current efforts to highlight civil society and the social economy as countervailing forces to the market view are a continuation of the historical struggle to reclaim the social dimension of economics.

What is the implication of all this for tax justice and the larger questions of unfairness and inequality in our economic system? Basically, it is that tax policies should be used to support economic models and institutions that distribute economic and social power more equitably. The support of co-operative enterprises and institutions is but one example.

A second approach is to consider how the practice of reciprocity itself is enhanced, particularly with respect to social welfare and the production of social and relational goods. This touches on the key questions of social care, the roles of government and the private sector, and most important, the role of the social economy as a repository of progressive values.

Conceiving a Social Market

To make any headway on this front, we must confront the dependence of civil society institutions on government. Civil society, despite its formal distinctions from the state, remains a dependent sector – in many ways a client sector of the state. Legions of non-profits and NGOs are utterly reliant on government funding. For example, more than 50 per cent of services provided by voluntary non-profit social welfare agencies in the United States are funded through government purchase-of-service arrangements. Government funding accounts for 65 per cent of the Catholic Charities budget and over 60 per cent of the Save the Children budget, as well as 96 per cent of the Volunteers of America budget.[18]

The same is true in Canada, and the resulting absence of autonomy has undermined these organizations' capacity to fight for the interests of civil society as a sector with its own interests separate from those of the state. At a time when government has all but erased the distinctions between the private and public sectors, this ongoing dependence is a fatal weakness that is allowing the interests of capital to continue their domination of public policy and to perpetuate an economic system that is subservient to their interests.

Never has this been more obvious. In Canada, it is evident in the dismantling of all constraints on capital, as evidenced by the gutting of environmental protections and of national regulatory powers with respect to the conduct of industry; in the promotion of corporate interests internationally under the guise of foreign aid (the corruption of CIDA); in the blocking of international progress on climate change; and in the undermining of the bargaining rights of labour. Meanwhile, the one sector of society that has the potential to defend the public interest and to push for progressive change has been effectively neutered by the state through this dependency. Because the Tides Foundation opposed the Conservative government's policy on the proposed Enbridge pipeline, it is being threatened with the removal of its charitable status. This impulse to silence criticism and to eradicate opposition is being institutionalized through the government's "review" of the political activities of charitable associations and their receipt of international funding. In the government's view, an organization that is granted charitable status relinquishes its civic rights.

But in this age of rampant privatization, the key area where civil society organizations need to reflect upon and articulate civic solutions relates to the protection of social goods. Social economy organizations must face up to the contradiction between their service to society and the betrayal of the public interest by governments. This will require the liberation of the social economy from its dependency on the state. It demands the maturation of the sector as an independent social and political force, and the creation of a true social market for social and relational goods – a social market, in other words, that is suited to the unique role of the social economy as a primary provider of these goods. Only in this way may the overwhelming power of the capitalist market be brought into balance with civic values.

An autonomous social economy based on reciprocity and civic values makes possible the political power necessary to negotiate a new social contract for a new reality. And this entails a wholly new perspective on how the principle of taxation – pooling capital for a social purpose – can be reinvented as a means whereby citizens and social economy organizations can mobilize capital to provide social goods in a way that is neither a means to generate profit, as current social investment schemes do, nor a form of dependency on state funding. This is particularly critical in the area of mobilizing new, civil forms of capital for social care.

What is really at issue is whether key actors and organizations within civil society and the social economy will be able to establish a consensus on the changed reality and on the need for civil society to play a new role – to in effect grow up and take its place as an autonomous sector of society in proper balance with the state and the private market. Until this happens, the galloping colonization of social and public space by capital will continue.

Civil society is the repository of those values and social relations that are best suited to the provision of care in a manner that is humane, responsive, and founded on reciprocity and mutuality – principles that are the hallmarks of caring relationships. What is lacking is the development of civil society institutions that are capable of applying these civic values on a scale, and in the context, of an economic and political reality that is daily undermining both their meaning and their relevance.

Tax policy can be a key means of protecting and promoting these values. To do so, it must recognize and reward reciprocity as a primary social good, it must understand that capital is *both* a social and a private good, and it must nurture the emergence of social markets that are attuned to the needs of the social economy. Taxation can be a powerful instrument that not only elevates the power and utility of civil society as a whole but also strengthens those institutions and practices which, through the democratic distribution of power, can help counteract the threat posed to social and economic justice by the domination of capital that we are witnessing in the present day.

Conclusion

The Way Out of This Mess

MURRAY DOBBIN

THIS BOOK IS ABOUT TAXES, but we recognize that this issue is just one of many critical ones facing advanced democracies like Canada. Where do the issues of taxes and adequate government revenue fit in the broad struggle against neoliberalism and the corporate state? Clearly, the radical reduction of taxes on the wealthy and corporations but also on the middle class was and is a key element of the Washington Consensus – the new elite consensus that emerged in the mid-1970s. But it is only one of several market-driven imperatives designed to dismantle the postwar Keynesian state.

We have argued in this book that governments of the past twenty years have (1) slashed taxes to deliberately reduce government's social and economic capacity; (2) systematically misled Canadians about the reasons for and real impact of tax cuts; and (3) through those cuts, helped create a level of inequality in Canada not seen since the 1920s. We have also argued that we can easily reverse this diminishing of Canadian democracy by increasing revenues through a return to fairer and more robust tax levels that increase the percentage of GDP devoted to public goods and services – that is, to the broad Canadian community.

With the election of a majority government led by right-wing libertarian Stephen Harper, the conjuncture of dramatic revenue losses and draconian cuts to government programs has taken on a new and ominous urgency. This no-longer-secret Harper agenda is the ground on which Canadians will fight the future battle of ideas over the appropriate level of taxes and their redistributive architecture. The Harper government's efforts to diminish the country are becoming obvious to more and more Canadians. It may well be that we have finally reached a kind of free market fatigue: that we are no longer willing to accept corporate and government propaganda about the benefits of tax cuts or the supposed need for 99 per cent of us to tighten our belts while the 1 per cent get to keep loosening theirs another notch.

The recent formation of a number of fair tax organizations – Canadians for Tax Fairness, Doctors for Fair Taxes, Lawyers for Fair Taxes, the Uncut movement, and others – speaks to the critical role that taxes and government revenues play in both neoliberalism and the resistance to it.

It could be argued that the dramatic reduction in government revenue as a percentage of GDP was a key element in the new project to place control of developed nations' economies and governance back in the hands of corporations. While other elements of the Washington Consensus (privatization, deregulation, free trade, labour "flexibility") were being implemented, the continued existence of a state with robust revenues always put the broader project at risk because the programs and services provided by state revenues retained their broad popularity. The persistence of these publicly funded and administered programs and services reminded people of the progressive role of government and undermined other elements of the neoliberal agenda.

As neoliberal "anti-governments" continue their gradual dismantling of democratic governance, the systematic starvation of the welfare state has become a final critical objective. If citizens can be persuaded that there is simply no more money in the kitty – if they can be deceived into believing that the reason for tax cuts is to boost the economy – then this strengthens all the other pieces of the neoliberal project. The old slogan from the free trade fight of the late 1980s comes into play once again: there is no alternative. The right – for example, Preston Manning's Centre for Building Democracy – claims that Canadians are becoming more individualistic, that they are pining for less government and eager to take on more personal responsibility.

The right seems to understand something that progressive forces haven't fully appreciated: that their claims about changing Canadian values are false. There is almost no evidence that Canadian progressive values have changed significantly – which demonstrates just how resilient those values are. But the right also understands that you don't actually have to change people's values – all you need to do is change their expectations. And at this, the right has been extremely successful.

As Diana Gibson points out in her chapter, much of the success of the right can be found in their careful strategic framing of messages that lower people's expectations of government. And it is not just the framing but also the adoption of identical messages by *all* the ideological agencies of the right: think tanks, academics, the media, business organizations, and pro-business political parties. This relentless cacophony of anti-government narrative has pounded the message home: expect less.

Among the core anti-government themes pursued by the right were free trade with the United States, the deficit hysteria of the early 1990s, the demonization of government employees (overpaid, underworked bureaucrats), and the disparaging of public services such as education and health care. Stephen Harper added to this by developing a fear-based security state (through crime bills and an aggressive military stance) and by conducting a multifaceted voter suppression strategy that made politics distasteful. All of these campaigns – both ideological and program-based – diminished people's expectations of and attachment to government as an expression of community.

The latest campaign, ramped up over the past twelve years, speaks directly to this question of fiscal capacity. The attack on taxes (Harper once claimed, "I don't believe that any taxes are good taxes") has been one of the most sustained and effective in the broad assault on democracy. The Canadian Taxpayers Federation started the campaign back in the 1980s with two provincial groups in Alberta and Saskatchewan, and Preston Manning and the Reform Party built on the populist appeal in their political strategy. Manning repeatedly used the image of the government with its hand in your pocket – as if government was actually stealing from its own people. Another frame that Manning used was the notion that individuals knew better how to spend their money than governments did.

To powerful effect, the "tax burden" and "tax relief" frames pose taxes as an affliction, implying that they are a kind of chronic illness in the lives of ordinary people. Those who offer relief from the burden are the good guys. It is not just the right's thorough framing of the tax issue that has made talking about taxes difficult; it is also the fact that there has been almost no counter-narrative from the left for a very long time. This means that the anti-tax messages are now deeply embedded in people's attitudes towards taxation.

Again, keep in mind that the tax issue – tax fairness and, just as important, ensuring sufficient revenue to accomplish progressive social and economic goals – is just one of the fronts on which we must challenge neoliberalism. So-called free trade deals are being signed every year; privatization through public/private partnerships continues to hand over public assets and services to private corporations; deregulation continues apace, especially regarding the environment.

But as important as all those issues are, none speak so directly to the positive role of government in maintaining the commons as the tax issue does. All roads lead inexorably to the fiscal capacity of the democratic state. Rooting our response to the right's destructive agenda in building a popular commitment to collectively pay for things we want to do together is critical to maintaining democratic governance. Unless we score a victory on this issue, winning battles on these other fronts will – still – leave us impoverished as a nation and as a community.

How can the progressive community engage in this project? First and foremost, it must have a consistent message on taxes, tax cuts, government revenues, and the services those revenues provide people. At the very least, this involves a careful and strategic reframing of the entire issue so that when we talk about taxes, and try to foment a national debate about them, we do so in the most effective manner possible. Given the dominance of the right's framing of the issue, it is easy to inadvertently reinforce their message even when we think we are delivering our own and our own values.

At this point in Canada, the kind of research and analysis that such an effective reframing requires hasn't been done yet. Because the task involves a multidisciplinary approach – one that encompasses sociology, psychology, linguistics, and other academic fields – the process is both time consuming and expensive.

Yet it is also clear that we cannot wait until we have the perfect message before we push back against the ongoing assault on government revenues, an assault that threatens all of the gains made in the postwar era of activist government. And indeed, the battle is already engaged. It seems that after many years of frustrating silence on the issue, the imperative to reclaim the commons by protecting its financial means of survival and growth has become obvious. Just in the past two years, many initiatives – some national, some provincial and local – have begun taking the message to the public (or their own publics): that taxes are the price we pay for a civilized society.

Doctors for Fair Taxation, Lawyers for Fair Taxation, and Faith Leaders for Fair Taxation have all formed in the past year or two. There is also a national group, Canadians for Tax Fairness (the publisher of this book), which is being funded by a broad range of labour and civil society groups that are now acutely aware of this issue's importance. Also, groups are beginning to form at the provincial level, such as Nova Scotians for Tax Fairness. The Canadian section of the international Uncut anti-austerity movement has at least fourteen local chapters across the country. NUPGE, the federation of provincial government employee unions, has been running a smart and well-resourced tax campaign called All Together Now for several years. The Canadian Labour Congress is developing its own program. Analyses of the issue are now being conducted, led by the national and B.C. offices of the Canadian Centre for Policy Alternatives.

While ideally, all of the above campaigns will have a similar core message – tying good government and its services to paying taxes – the multiplicity of voices is itself an encouraging sign. Add to this the occasional (though still too infrequent) dissenting message from the Canadian political and economic elites and the potential base for a progressive tax movement looks to be quite broad. For a brief moment in 2010 even John Manley, the head of the Canadian Council of Chief Executives (formerly the BCNI), spoke out publicly for the need for robust public revenues and tax increases on high-income Canadians. Apparently even those who have spent years clamouring for tax cuts seem to realize that to remain "internationally competitive," a country actually has to have roads, bridges, schools, and hospitals.

While more and more unions are coming on board the tax fairness campaign, it is critical that the coalition or network include a much broader range of civil society groups – the cultural sector, the environmental movement, the student movement, the anti-poverty, seniors, and human rights movements. Also, those among the elite who clearly do not support the radical libertarian agenda need to add their voices. No matter what the specific fight for social justice, its ultimate success depends on government revenue.

The critical loss of government revenues is not confined to the federal government: provincial administrations have been almost as eager to jettison money by reducing taxes on upper-income earners and corporations. All three levels of government are ripe for tax reform messages, especially including municipalities, whose spending burdens continue to grow as a result of downloading from senior levels even while their taxing powers become increasingly inadequate. And all political parties are ripe for a strong campaign, for all of them, including the NDP, have in the past fifteen years accepted the tax cut mantra.

Despite a hostile media environment and a twenty-year head start on the issue by the right, the prospects for building support for the goal of fairer taxes and robust revenues have never been better. Many polls reveal that we are prepared to pay more. A 2012 Ekos poll found that 59 per cent of Canadians chose investing in social programs as the highest government priority, compared to 16 per cent who wanted to keep taxes as low as possible.

Polling also demonstrates that Canadians recognize the progressive role that taxes can play regarding an increasingly important issue: inequality. The Broadbent Institute's spring 2012 polling revealed that 77 per cent identified inequality as a major problem undermining Canadian values and that they were willing to do their part to address it and believed it should be a government priority. A large percentage supported fairer taxes (with the wealthy and corporations paying more), and a significant majority – 64 per cent – were willing to pay more themselves to save social programs. Seventy-two per cent of Liberal and NDP supporters and even 58 per cent of Conservative supporters were willing to pay more. The majority support held across regions, gender, age, education level, and family income.

In 2012, when the provincial NDP in Ontario called for a modest 2 per cent tax hike for those earning half a million dollars or more, the public response was overwhelmingly in favour, by a margin of 78 per cent in favour to 17 per cent opposed. Even in Calgary – in the heart of anti-tax country – 55 per cent supported increasing municipal taxes while only 10 per cent called for a decrease. A poll commissioned by the International Trade Union Confederation in thirteen countries, most of them members of the G20, found that an average of 63 per cent of respondents supported a financial transactions tax. Canada was well above the average at 74 per cent support.

The media – whose role in demonizing taxes has been powerful – has been caught off guard by these and other polls. The *Globe and Mail* did an interactive poll the day before the 2012 federal budget and declared its shock: "What stood out was the across the board call for higher taxes." People were willing to see the GST restored to 7 per cent. A columnist for the *National Post* worried that the arguments against taxing the wealthy were not very convincing.

The polling results of the last year are encouraging and reinforce results that have been observed over the years. Canadians have consistently supported higher taxes, but only if they are assured that the increased revenue will be spent on progressive programs. When the tax increase is tied to health care, education, poverty reduction, child care, and so on, significant majorities support tax increases. This is encouraging; however, it also shows that a general distrust in government is a major barrier to actually achieving tax fairness and adequate government revenues.

As the Frameworks Institute, the foremost American issue-framing group, states in the conclusion to its U.S. tax reframing project:

> More than framing is needed to reverse entrenched patterns of thinking. While framing is essential to growing a more fruitful dialog about budgets and taxes, it is insufficient to solve the problem of passivity. Only citizen engagement can do that. Agency, transparency and participation in the process are all lacking and all are necessary preconditions for reframing budgets and taxes. When citizens in our peer discourse sessions were engaged with the complex tasks of both developing a budget and raising the funds to support it, they became more engaged, less critical of government, and more supportive of the product they had made. . . . While framing can help to lessen the "othering" effect of government vs. us, it can only be resolved long-term if people have familiarity with doing government.

Let us assume that Canadians are similarly more likely to support government when they are more engaged in democratic practices. This suggests a high bar for progressive politics in Canada. What is it about the way we do politics that leaves people disengaged? And what would progressives have to do to create a different, more engaging way of organizing?

Part of the answer is to frame the issue as a choice between two very different futures: one, a continuation of the dystopian low-tax, high-private-consumption regime; the other, a return to higher taxes but also to more public goods and stronger communities. A model for the former has existed for many years south of the border, and it is one that Canadians are acutely aware of. Models for the latter certainly exist in the Nordic countries, but their political cultures are profoundly different from ours. Citizens in the Nordic countries are more politically literate and engaged in the democratic governance of their societies than Canadians are. In Sweden, the government subsidizes hundreds of thousands of political study groups, and citizens emerge from these deeply informed and with a high regard for government and its role in their lives.

This suggests that we need to rethink the model of social change we have been using for more than forty years: a model based on single-issue organizations, sometimes referred to as issue "silos" – organizations fighting for medicare, child care, the environment, poverty reduction, affordable secondary education, or even fair taxes. It's a long list.

This model for social change organizing was formed in the early 1970s at a time when governments actually believed in democratic governance and the nation-state and genuinely engaged with civil society groups. Those groups pressured governments on policy matters and even offered expert advice on the social policy areas they focused on. It was by no means a perfect relationship, but there was a genuine dialogue. Today governments are shamelessly dismantling what previous governments built – they don't want policy advice, and unless a movement is strong enough to actually threaten a governing party's power, they have no intention of responding even to majority opinion.

I am not suggesting that single-issue organizations have been ineffective. Far from it – had they not been active, things would be immeasurably worse, and medicare, for example, would be well down the road to privatization. But it is clear that these groups are now, for the most part, shadows of their former selves, exhausted from their efforts to have an impact on right-wing governments and finding it more difficult to sign up members and motivate them to act. The major exceptions are environmental groups, the Enbridge pipeline issue being the obvious example.

Reclaiming the commons through a broad-based movement will not be easy. Two momentous developments illustrate the need to reinvent social change movements: Occupy and the Quebec student rebellion. These two share something extraordinary and potentially transformational: they see themselves as creating community and are marked not just by anger at injustice and inequality but by an outpouring of joy at discovering their newly created community spirit.

The Occupy movement's creating of new communities (with libraries, day care, kitchens, and medical clinics at their sites) is well known. So, too, is that movement's nurturing, positive spirit. The Quebec "Casseroles" rebellion (named after the nightly, spirited banging of pots in communities across Quebec) was imbued with that same spirit. "It is not a movement of anger, of rage or of hate," writes journalist Ethan Cox. "It is a movement of love, of community, and of hope. People who would be alone in their houses watching TV take to the streets and march with neighbours they never knew they had."

This reconnecting of progressive politics with community is up against twenty years of culture wars that have made Canada more individualistic and less communitarian than it was in the postwar years. As community is undermined and diminished, people have little choice but to engage with the new world as they encounter it. Meanwhile, consumerism has become rampant and the marketing and advertising of an endless array of goods and services ever more sophisticated and manipulative. And while the seductions of the marketplace with its range of enticing goodies have increased, the appeal of the commons has steadily decreased. Because of ongoing cuts to public services and the business model that has been applied to them, people feel they have less connection with many public services than they do with the private marketplace. The distinction between private goods for customers and public goods for "clients" (rather than citizens) has been blurred.

Yet the economic crisis, the record levels of private debt, and the seemingly permanent increase in economic insecurity may turn out to be the kind of "useful crisis" for the left that the right has become famous for exploiting. If the private marketplace cannot provide economic security, there is only one other option. To date, those who promote tax cuts have been able to exploit the fact that incomes for the vast majority of Canadian workers have been flat since the early 1980s. It is easy to argue in these circumstances that the only way you can increase your disposable income is through lowered taxes.

Yet the polling referred to above suggests that Canadians' experience is starting to trump the private-market propaganda regarding the role of government. Erosions to social programs and the prospect of more and more cuts to government spending have heightened popular awareness of the difference between private and public goods. And the relationship between taxes and public goods is clearly on the minds of most citizens.

Those who support fair and robust taxes are wise to continually connect them to the government services they receive – indeed, some campaigners suggest talking about taxes only secondarily once the issue of declining services has already been broached. Such is the distance we have to go in order to overcome the anti-tax sentiment. Yet in Canada, at least in the era of Occupy, questions of taxes are clearly tied in people's minds to issues of inequality. They understand there is considerable overlap here, in that the provision of well-funded services does contribute directly to greater equality.

Campaigning for fair taxes and more robust government only makes sense in the context of progressive government. The message has to be consistent with other progressive messages and campaigns. Increasing tax revenues in the context of a majority Harper Conservative government would simply facilitate, for example, that government's commitment to virtually doubling military spending over the next twenty years and to the building of new prisons.

It is equally important that the tax message be persuasive in its substance. People need to know that the progressive tax proponents have done their homework, that the taxes they propose or propose to increase will accomplish the things they say they will and not have the adverse effects claimed by the tax cutters. The chapters in this book contribute to that substantive argument. Jim Stanford convincingly debunks the myth that tax cuts for corporations stimulate economic growth and spur new investment – one of the principal arguments of those calling for ever more tax cuts.

Toby Sanger makes a compelling case for a financial transactions tax – the so-called Robin Hood Tax – and demonstrates just how easy it would be to raise tens of billions of dollars for the public good in a way that has virtually no negative impact on real productive investment. Of all the examples of unfairness in the system, tax havens must top the list. The world's largest corporations and wealthiest individuals stash literally trillions of dollars in offshore banks, thereby making themselves immune to taxation and robbing governments of hundreds of billions in revenues. As Peter Gillespie points out, there is simply no argument, moral or economic, that can possibly justify this blatant thievery. Shutting down these criminal operations would free up enormous sums of money that could be devoted to public services and greater equality.

Taxes produce revenues for services, infrastructure, and income redistribution; they can also encourage certain publicly beneficial behaviours while discouraging others. This is the role of eco-taxes, the focus of Joe Gunn's chapter. The market, left on its own, tilts towards antisocial behaviour as corporations try to externalize as many of their costs as possible. We are already familiar with – and supportive of – taxes that counter this market trend. An example is tobacco taxes, which prevent tobacco companies from externalizing the huge health costs of smoking and provide a powerful disincentive for people to smoke at all.

All of the detailed work on how, exactly, to achieve the revenue we need, fairly and equitably, must still be put in the context of communitarian values. As Trish Hennessy argues in her chapter: "A tax is the gift generations of social citizens hand down, one to the other." Getting people to think differently about taxes – and government – may still be the most important goal and biggest challenge of the next decade.

In the end, it is what progressives propose to spend fairer and higher taxes *on* that will determine the outcome of the national conversation on taxes that is so desperately needed. A vision of strong social programs, additional programs such as child care, economic security, mobilizing to deal with climate change, and a reclaiming of the commons must all lead the conversation. When they do, public support for fair taxes will be inevitable.

Notes

Introduction: Tax Fairness Key to Rebuilding Canada

1 "Canada through Stephen Harper's Eyes," Speech to Council for National Policy conference in Montreal, 1997. thetyee.ca/News/2011/03/23/StephenHarpersEyes.
2 "Statement by the Prime Minister of Canada at the World Economic Forum," pm.gc.ca/eng/media.asp?id=4604.
3 Ben Sand and Peter Shawn Taylor, "Harper's Tax Boutique: Rethinking Tax Expenditures in a Time of Deficit," Frontier Centre for Public Policy, March 2011, www.fcpp.org/files/1/FB091_PSTMiddle_F3.pdf.
4 "Parliamentary Budget Office Economic and Fiscal Outlook 2012," p. 32, www.parl.gc.ca/PBO-DPB/documents/EFO_April_2012.pdf.
5 "Government stimulus measures too feeble: Stiglitz," www.theglobeandmail.com/report-on-business/economy/government-stimulus-measures-too-feeble-stiglitz/article4183548.
6 Tax Justice Network, "The Cost of Tax Abuse," November 2011, www.tackletaxhavens.com/Cost_of_Tax_Abuse_TJN_Research_23rd_Nov_2011.pdf.
7 Statistics Canada, "Foreign Direct Investment Positions, 2011" www.statcan.gc.ca/daily-quotidien/120419/t120419b001-eng.htm.
8 Statistics Canada, "Foreign Direct Investment, 2011," www.statcan.gc.ca/daily-quotidien/120419/dq120419b-eng.htm.
9 Canadian Centre for Policy Alternatives, Marc Lee, "Fair and Effective Carbon Pricing – Lessons from BC," February 2011, p. 16, www.policyalternatives.ca/sites/default/files/uploads/publications/BC%20Office/2011/02/CCPA-BC_Fair_Effective_Carbon_SUMMARY_2.pdf.
10 Sustainable Prosperity, "British Columbia's Carbon Tax Shift: The First Four Years," www.sustainableprosperity.ca/article2864.
11 Centre for the Study of Living Standards, "The Impact of Redistribution on Income Inequality in Canada and the Provinces, 1981–2010," September 2012, www.csls.ca/reports/csls2012-08.pdf.
12 Monica Townson, "CCPA Policy Brief: A Stronger Foundation, Pension Reform and Old Age Security," November 2009. www.policyalternatives.ca/sites/default/files/uploads/publications/reports/docs/Stronger_Foundation.pdf

1 Passing on the Torch

1 www.crfa.ca/research.
2 www.thestar.com/opinion/article/715565-can-we-have-an-adult-conversation-about-taxes.
3 www.environicsinstitute.org/PDF-Citizenship-Rpt-EN.pdf.
4 www.broadbentinstitute.ca/sites/default/files/uploaded-manually/equality-project.pdf.
5 www.environicsinstitute.org/PDF-FocusCanada-2011-Final.pdf.
6 www.cbc.ca/news/politics/story/2012/05/03/former-prime-ministers.html.

2 Pushing the Envelope

1 CBC, *Canada A People's History,* www.cbc.ca/history/EPISCONTENTSE1EP13CH2PA1LE.html.
2 Lewis F. Powell, Jr., "Confidential Memorandum: Attack on American Free Enterprise System," personal memorandum to Mr. Eugene B. Sydnor, Jr., Chairman, Education Committee, U.S. Chamber of Commerce, August 23, 1971.
3 Ibid.
4 CBC News, "Harper Defends Remarks to U.S. Conservative Movement," January 12, 2006, www.cbc.ca/story/canadavotes2006/national/2006/01/12/harper-quotes060112.html#ixzz21fRlC0WR.
5 For more on the Overton window, visit the Mackinac Centre website, www.mackinac.org/7504.
6 Stephen Ducat, "Post-Reality Politics, Part One: Down the Rabbit Hole with the New GOP," *Huffington Post,* July 5, 2011, www.huffingtonpost.com/stephen-ducat/gop-2012-candidates_b_890004.html.
7 Jeffrey Simpson, "A Very Scary PM: 'I Don't Believe That Any Taxes Are Good Taxes,'" *Globe and Mail,* July 13, 2009.
8 William A. Gamson and Charlotte Ryan, "Thinking About Elephants: Toward a Dialogue with George Lakoff," *Public Eye,* Fall 2005.
9 Lewis H. Lapham, "Tentacles of Rage: The Republican Propaganda Mill: A Brief History," *Harper's,* September 2004.
10 Jacob S. Hacker and Paul Pierson, "Winner-Take-All Politics: Public Policy, Political Organization, and the Precipitous Rise of Top Incomes in the United States," *Politics and Society* 38 (2010): 176.
11 Dennis Gruending, "Conservative Think Tanks Multiply in Canada," *Straight Goods,* October 21, 2007.

12 Marci McDonald, *The Armageddon Factor: The Rise of Christian Nationalism in Canada* (Toronto: Random House, 2010).

13 Hacker and Pierson, "Winner-Take-All Politics."

14 David Macdonald, Canadian Centre for Policy Alternatives, "Corporate Income Taxes, Profit, and Employment Performance of Canada's Largest Companies," April 6, 2011.

15 Ibid.

16 Armine Yalnizyan, Canadian Centre for Policy Alternatives, "The Rise of Canada's Richest 1%," December 2010.

17 Andrew G. Berg and Jonathan D. Ostry, International Monetary Fund, "Equality and Efficiency: Is There a Trade-Off Between the Two or Do They Go Hand in Hand?", *Finance and Development* 48, no. 3 (September 2011), www.imf.org/external/pubs/ft/fandd/2011/09/Berg.htm

18 There is a large field of research on inequality as a key social determinant of health. See Public Health Agency of Canada, "What Makes Canadians Health or Unhealthy?", www.phac-aspc.gc.ca/ph-sp/determinants/determinants-eng.php #defining; and R.G. Wilkinson, *The Impact of Inequality: How to Make Sick Societies Healthier* (London: Routledge, 2005).

19 Paul Krugman, "Missing Richard Nixon," *New York Times,* August 30, 2009.

3 The Power of Conventional Thinking

1 Nick Fillmore, "*Globe*'s Pro-Business Reporting Example of Bad Journalism," January 14, 2010, www.rabble.ca.

2 Tax Freedom Day, en.wikipedia.org/wiki/Tax_Freedom_Day.

3 taxpayer.com/federal/13th-annual.

4 Larry Patriquin, *Inventing Tax Rage: Misinformation in the* National Post (Halifax: Fernwood Publishing, 2004).

5 Thaddeus Hwong, "How Canada's Flat Tax Debate Played in the Press," *Tax Notes International*, March 2, 2009.

6 Bill Wasik, "Dismal Beat: The March of Personal Finance Journalism," *Harper's Magazine,* March 2003.

7 Emily Mills, "Risky Business," *Ryerson Review of Journalism,* Summer 2005.

8 Fillmore, "*Globe*'s Pro-Business Reporting."

9 Andrew Coyne, "Dalton McGuinty and His Liberal Tax Grab," *Maclean's*, April 16, 2009.

10 Wallace Immen, "Tories Launch Bid to Speed Up Immigration for Entrepreneurs," *Globe and Mail,* April 25, 2012.

11 "Norwood Family Office CEO Outlines Why Canada Is a Premier Destination for Wealthy Families Looking to Protect and Build Family Wealth," *PR Web,* October 20, 2010.

12 Terence Corcoran, "In Canada We Have No Conservatives," *Financial Post,* May 3, 2011.

13 Andrew Coyne, "Canada's Left-Wing, Unconservative, Compromise-Ridden Conservatives," *National Post,* April 12, 2009.

14 John Moore, "Fox to 'Balance' Canada's Right-Wing Media Bias," *National Post,* June 15, 2010.

15 Hwong, "How Canada's Flat Tax Debate Played in the Press."

4 The Trouble with Tax Havens

1 John Christensen, "The Hidden Trillions: Secrecy, Corruption, and the Offshore Interface," *Crime, Law, Social Change* 57 (2012): 325–43.

2 Canada, *House of Commons,* Standing Committee on Finance, March 3, 2011.

3 United Nations Office of Drugs and Crime, "Estimating Illicit Financial Flows Resulting from Drug Trafficking and Other Transnational Organized Crime," Vienna, October 2011.

4 Robert Lacey, *Little Man: Meyer Lansky and the Gangster Life* (Boston: Little, Brown, 1991).

5 Ibid., 29.

6 R.T. Naylor, *Hot Money and the Politics of Debt* (Montreal: Black Rose Books, 1994), 21.

7 Ibid., 22.

8 Margaret Beare and Stephen Schneider, *Money Laundering in Canada* (Toronto: University of Toronto Press, 2007).

9 Catherine Wismer, *Sweethearts: The Builders, the Mob, and the Men* (Toronto: James Lorimer, 1980), 117.

10 Nicholas Shaxson, *Treasure Islands* (London: The Bodley Head, 2011), 103.

11 Ibid., 107.

12 Jeffrey Robinson, *The Sink* (Toronto: McClelland and Stewart, 2003), 67.

13 Shaxson, *Treasure Islands,* 103.

14 Ibid., 101.

15 David Chaikin, "Policy and Fiscal Effects of Swiss Bank Secrecy," *Revenue Law Journal* 15, no. 1 (2005). Chaikin notes that Swiss bank secrecy has a long tradition but that it was not until 1934 that bank confidentiality was made the subject of criminal sanctions. A myth promulgated by Swiss banks was that criminal sanctions were meant to protect Jewish assets from the Nazis. Actually, sanctions

were enacted after elite members of French society were caught evading taxes by using Swiss banking services.

16 Christensen, "The Hidden Trillions," 15.

17 James Henry, "The Price of Offshore Revisited," *Tax Justice Network,* July 2012, www.taxjustice.net.

18 CBC News, "Offshore Bank Account Probe Nets Canadians," September 30, 2010, www.cbc.ca/news/canada/story/2010/09/29/tax-account-hsbc.html.

19 Robinson, *The Sink*, 94.

20 Leo-Paul Lauzon and Marc Hasbani, "Les Banques Canadiennes et l'évasion Fiscale dans les paradis fiscaux, 1993–2007," Université du Québec à Montréal, Mai 2008.

21 Trevor Cole, "How I Learned to Avoid the Taxman in the British Virgin Islands," *Globe and Mail*, January 27, 2011.

22 U.S. GAO, "International Taxation: Large U.S. Corporations and Federal Contractors with Subsidiaries in Jurisdictions Listed as Tax Havens or Financial Privacy Jurisdictions," GAO-09–157, December 2008.

23 Citizens for Tax Justice, "Big No-Tax Corps Just Keep on Dodging," April 9, 2012, ctj.org/mt/mt-search.cgi?search=general+electric+tax+&IncludeBlogs=7&limit=20

24 Jesse Drucker, "Google 2.4% Rate Shows How $60 Billion Lost to Tax Loopholes," *Bloomberg*, October 21, 2010, www.bloomberg.com/news/2010-10-21/google-2-4-rate-shows-how-60-billion-u-s-revenue-lost-to-tax-loopholes.html.

25 Elizabeth Poe, "Corporate Tax Evasion Sends US Dollars and Jobs Overseas," *Washington Times*, October 12, 2011, communities.washingtontimes.com/neighborhood/ad-lib/2011/oct/12/corporate-tax-evasion-sends-us-dollars-and-jobs-ov.

26 Citizens for Tax Justice, "Loopholes for Sale: Campaign Contributions by Corporate Tax Dodgers," March 2012, www.ctj.org/loopholesforsale.

27 Floor Statement on the introduction of *Stop Tax Haven Abuse Act*, Senator Carl Levin, U.S. Senate, July 12, 2011.

28 Richard Murphy, "Tax Justice and Jobs: The Business Case for Investing in Staff at HM Revenue and Customs," Tax Research LLP (London: March 2010), www.taxresearch.org.uk/Documents/PCSTaxGap.pdf.

29 Canada, Report of the Auditor General of Canada, Ottawa, December 2002, Chapter 11, 17.

30 Statistics Canada, "Foreign Direct Investment Positions, 2011," www.statcan.gc.ca/daily-quotidien/120419/t120419b001-eng.htm.

31 Global Financial Integrity, "Illicit Financial Flows from Developing Countries, 2000–2009," Washington, 2011, iff-update.gfintegrity.org.

32 Global Financial Integrity, "Illicit Financial Flows from Africa: Hidden Resource for Development," Washington, 2010, www.gfintegrity.org/content/view/300/154.

33 Léonce Ndikumana and James Boyce, *Africa's Odious Debts: How Foreign Loans and Capital Flight Bled a Continent* (London: Zed Books, 2011).

34 Ibid., 47.

35 Ibid., 83.

36 Christian Aid, "Death and Taxes: The True Toll of Tax Dodging," May 2008, www.christianaid.org.uk/images/deathandtaxes.pdf.

37 Global Financial Integrity, "Illicit Financial Flows from the Least Developed Countries, 1990–2008," Washington, 2011, www.gfintegrity.org/content/view/374/70.

38 Maria de Boyrie, James Nelson, and Simon J. Pak, "Capital Movement Through Trade Mis-Invoicing: The Case of Africa," *Journal of Financial Crime* 14, no. 4 (2007): 474–89.

39 United Nations Office on Drugs and Crime and the World Bank, "Stolen Asset Recovery (StAR) Initiative: Challenges, Opportunities, and Action Plan," Washington, 2007, siteresources.worldbank.org/NEWS/Resources/Star-rep-full.pdf

40 Ibid., 5.

41 Tax Justice Network, "Tax Havens Cause Poverty," last modified 2002, www.taxjustice.net/cms/front_content.php?idcatart=2&lang=1.

42 Raymond Baker, speech: "The Ugliest Chapter in Global Economic Affairs Since Slavery,'" 2007, www.gfintegrity.org/content/view/109/74.

43 Leaders' Statement, G20 Summit, London, April 2, 2009, 4, g20.org/images/stories /canalfinan/docs/uk/07finalcomu.pdf.

44 Christensen, *The Hidden Trillions*, 335.

45 Tax Justice Network, "Financial Secrecy Index, 2011," last modified 2011, www.financialsecrecyindex.com/index.html.

46 Robinson, *The Sink*, 70.

47 Alain Deneault, *Offshore: Tax Havens and the Rule of Global Crime* (New York: The New Press, 2011), 93.

48 Christensen, *The Hidden Trillions*, 335.

5 The Failure of Corporate Tax Cuts to Stimulate Business Investment Spending

The material in this chapter is based on research originally published by the Canadian Centre for Policy Alternatives. See Jim Stanford, *Having Their Cake and Eating It Too: Business Profits, Taxes, and Investment in Canada, 1961 Through 2010* (Ottawa: 2011).

1 Bradford DeLong and Lawrence Summers, "Equipment Investment and Economic Growth," *Quarterly Journal of Economics* 106, no. 2 (1991): 445–502.

2 Jim Stanford, *Economics for Everyone: A Short Guide to the Economics of Capitalism* (Ottawa: Canadian Centre for Policy Alternatives, 2008), Ch. 12.

3 Someshwar Rao, Jianmin Tang, and Wiemin Wang, "Canada's Recent Productivity Record and Capital Accumulation," *International Productivity Monitor* 7 (Fall 2003): 24–38; Andrew Sharpe, "The Relationship Between ICT Investment and Productivity in the Canadian Economy: A Review of the Evidence," Centre for the Study of Living Standards, Research Report 2006–05.

4 According to data published by the Canada Revenue Agency, two-thirds of all taxable dividend income, and three-quarters of all taxable capital gains, were received by tax filers with income in excess of $100,000 in 2008 (a group that represents just over 5 per cent of all tax filers). See Department of Finance Canada (2010), *Canada's Economic Action Plan Report #6*, September.

5 The data in Figure 1 are retrieved from Statistics Canada's investment intentions survey; the data in Figure 2 come from the national income accounts. Methodological differences between the two sources explain why investment is a lower apparent share of GDP in Figure 2 than in Figure 1.

6 The capital consumption allowance (CCA) represents charges that are deducted from a company's profits to reflect the wear-and-tear of existing capital but that are not paid in actual cash. Hence a company's cash flow is not reduced by CCA charges, only its reported profits.

7 Business investments in non-tangible assets have also declined during this period. For example, business R&D expenditures in Canada have declined by about one-third as a share of GDP since 2001.

8 Governments in B.C. and Ontario have recently announced that planned reductions in corporate tax rates will be postponed as part of deficit reduction strategies.

9 Because of sharp fluctuations in before-tax profits (such as those associated with recessions and recoveries), this estimate of the effective tax rate can fluctuate significantly even without any changes in tax policy, but the longer-run average is still a reasonable measure of the ongoing effective tax burden on business.

10 The increase in the apparent effective tax rate in 2010 is an anomaly reflecting the sharp decline in 2009 business profits associated with the recession; in this case, our method of relating taxes paid to previous year's profits produces a misleading estimate.

11 Note that the period of time covered by each sub-period does not correspond to the period of time each government was in office; it corresponds, rather, to the period of time until the next successive tax reform was implemented.

12 Note that most of the 2008–10 period covered by the Harper era we have defined, consisted of the 2008–09 recession and subsequent slow recovery (when business profits shrank). This average level of profits, therefore, understates the underlying structural improvement in before-tax profits; prior to the recession, before-tax profits reached 16 per cent of GDP – the highest in Canadian history, and a peak increase of over 4 percentage points of GDP compared to the pre-reform average (rather than the 1 point increase reported in Table 1).

13 Again, the recession pulled down these averages for the 2008–10 Harper era, and hence understate the improvement in longer-run profitability and cash flow.

14 Bank of Canada Governor Mark Carney recently referred to this idle corporate cash reserve as "dead money," sparking a badly needed public discussion of the issue.

15 The total stock of liquid assets held by non-financial businesses in Canada was almost half a trillion dollars at the end of 2010. Businesses typically require a normal stock of cash and liquid assets to conduct their affairs, however, so we have defined the "excess" as only the amount corresponding to the increase in the share of liquid assets as a proportion of GDP, compared to pre-2001 averages.

16 Stanford, *Having Their Cake and Eating It Too*.

17 The relationship was significant at the 10 per cent level in the full period, but not in the before- or after-reform sub-periods.

18 That is, higher taxes led to lower investment, and vice versa.

19 As investigated by Steven M. Fazzari, R. Glenn Hubbard, and Bruce Petersen, "Investment, Financing Decisions, and Tax Policy," *American Economic Review* 78, no. 3 (1988): 200–5; and, in a Canadian context, by Huntley Schaller, "Asymmetric Information, Liquidity Constraints, and Canadian Investment," *Canadian Journal of Economics* 26, no. 3 (1993): 552–74.

20 Equal to prime corporate lending rates less the year-over-year growth in consumer prices in Canada.

21 Stuart Landon and Constance E. Smith, "The Exchange Rate and Machinery and Equipment Imports. Identifying the Impact of Import Source and Export Destination Country Currency Valuation Changes," *North American Journal of Economics and Finance* 18, no 1 (2007): 3–21.

22 Stacey Tevlin and Karl Whelan, "Explaining the Investment Boom of the 1990s," *Journal of Money, Credit, and Banking* 35, no. 1 (2003): 1–22.

23 See Walid Hejazi and P. Pauly, "Motivations for FDI and Domestic Capital Formation," *Journal of International Business Studies* 34, no. 3 (2003): 282–89; Someshwar Rao, Malick Souare, and Weimin Wang, "The Economics of FDI: A Canadian Perspective," *Transnational Corporations Review* 1, no. 4 (2009): 28–41; and Andreas Waldkirch and Ayca Tekin-Coru, "North American Integration and Cana-

dian Foreign Direct Investment," *B.E. Journal of Economic Analysis and Policy* 10, no. 1 (2010): 1–38.

24 This finding is in line with the findings of other studies, such as Jason Cummins, Kevin Hassett, and Glenn Hubbard, "Tax Reforms and Investment: A Cross-Country Comparison," *Journal of Public Economics* 62, nos. 1–2 (1996): 237–73; and Jim Stanford, *Paper Boom: Why Real Prosperity Requires a New Approach to Canada's Economy* (Ottawa: Canadian Centre for Policy Alternatives and James Lorimer & Co., 1999), 164.

25 This effect results from the spinoff impact of construction projects on upstream supply purchases and downstream consumer spending. Department of Finance Canada (2010), Table A.1, 142.

26 Hadi Salehi Esfahani and Maria Teresa Ramirez, "Institutions, Infrastructure, and Economic Growth," *Journal of Development Economics* 70, no. 2 (2003): 443–77; Pantelis Kalaitzidakis and Sarantis Kalyvitis, "'New' Public Investment and/or Public Capital Maintenance for Growth? The Canadian Experience," *Economic Inquiry* 43, no. 3 (2005): 586–600.

6 Financial Transaction Taxes

1 John Maynard Keynes, *The General Theory of Employment, Interest and Money* (Cambridge: Cambridge University Press, 1935), Ch. 12, Section 5. Also at www.marxists.org/reference/subject/ics/keynes/general-theory/ch12.htm.

2 James Tobin, "A Proposal for International Monetary Reform," *Eastern Economic Journal* 4, nos. 3–4 (1978): 153–59. college.holycross.edu/RePEc/eej/Archive/Volume4/V4N3_4P153_159.pdf.

3 Madhavi Acharya-Tom Yew (2010). "Flaherty: No Bank Tax for Canada," *Toronto Star*, April 21, 2010, www.thestar.com/business/bank/article/798599-flaherty-no-bank-tax-for-canada.

4 European Commission, "Taxation of the Financial Sector: Frequently Asked Questions," ec.europa.eu/taxation_customs/taxation/other_taxes/financial_sector/index_en.htm.

5 Innovative Financing to Fund Development: Leading Group, "Globalizing Solidarity: The Case for Financial Levies," July 2010, www.leadinggroup.org/IMG/pdf_Financement_innovants_web_def.pdf.

6 Toby Sanger, *Fair Shares: How Banks, Brokers, and the Financial Industry Can Pay Fairer Taxes* (Ottawa: Canadian Centre for Policy Alternatives, 2011), 25.

7 Dean Baker, "The Deficit-Reducing Potential of a Financial Speculation Tax," Centre for Economic and Policy Research, January 2011, www.cepr.net/documents/publications/fst-2011–01.pdf.

8 International Monetary Fund, "Financial Sector Taxation: The IMF's Report to the G-20 and Background Material," September 2010, 20, www.imf.org/external/np/seminars/eng/2010/paris/pdf/090110.pdf.

9 Thomas Philippon, "The Evolution of the US Financial Industry from 1860 to 2007: Theory and Evidence," working paper, November 2008, economics.stanford.edu/files/Philippon5_20.pdf; idem, "Are Bankers Overpaid?", 2008, sternfinance.blogspot.ca/2008/11/are-banker-over-paid-thomas-philippon.html.

10 Olivier Baube, "World Economic Forum Davos 2012: David Cameron Slams Europe's Transaction Tax Plan," AFP, January 27, 2012.

11 European Commission, Macroeconomic Effects Technical Fiche, May 2012, ec.europa.eu/taxation_customs/taxation/other_taxes/financial_sector/index_en.htm.

12 Dean Baker and Helene Jorgensen, "The Relationship Between Financial Transactions Costs and economic Growth," Centre for economic and Policy Research, March 2012, www.cepr.net/index.php/publications/reports/the-relationship-between-financial-transactions-costs-and-ic-growth.

13 William Barker and Anna Pomeranets, "The Growth of High-Frequency Trading: Implications for Financial Stability," *Bank of Canada Financial System Review,* June 2011, 47–52, www.bankofcanada.ca/wp-content/uploads/2011/12/fsr-0611-barker.pdf.

14 Joseph P. Kennedy II, "The High Cost of Gambling on Oil," *New York Times*, April 10, 2012, www.nytimes.com/2012/04/11/opinion/ban-pure-speculators-of-oil-futures.html; Kevin G. Hall and Robert A. Rankin, "Speculation Explains More About Oil Prices Than Anything Else," May 13, 2012, www.mcclatchydc.com/2011/05/13/114190/speculation-explains-more-about.html.

15 Luciana Juvenal and Ivan Petrella, "Speculation in the Oil Market," Federal Reserve Bank of St. Louis Working Paper 2011–027C, October 2011, research.stlouisfed.org/wp/2011/2011-027.pdf.

16 Bernie Sanders, "Wall Street Greed Fueling High Gas Prices", *CNN Opinion,* February 28, 2012, www.cnn.com/2012/02/28/opinion/sanders-gas-speculation/index.html.

17 Baker and Jorgensen, "The Relationship."

18 Robin Hood Tax, "Everything You Need to Know," robinhoodtax.org/how-it-works/everything-you-need-to-know.

19 Algirdas Semeta, European Tax Commissioner (2012), "The Financial Transactions Tax: Europe Needs It," *World Commerce Review*, March 2012, www.worldcommercereview.com/publications/article_pdf/599.

20 International Monetary Fund, "Taxing Financial Transactions: Issues and Evidence," IMF Working Paper, 2011, 23, www.imf.org/external/pubs/ft/wp/2011/wp1154.pdf.

21 European Commission, "Technical Fiche: Tax Contribution of the Financial Sector," May 2012, ec.europa.eu/taxation_customs/resources/documents/taxation/other_taxes/financial_sector/fact_sheet/tax-contribution-fin-sector.pdf.

22 Kenneth Markle and Douglas Shackelford, "Cross-country Comparisons of Corporate Income Taxes," New York University School of Law Colloquium on Tax Policy, March 2010, Table 4, 45, www.law.nyu.edu/ecm_dlv3/groups/public/@nyu_law_web-site_academics_colloquia_tax_policy/documents/documents/ecm_pro_065293.pdf.

23 Leo-Paul Lauzon and Marc Hasbani, "Les banques Canadiennes et l'evasion fiscale dans les paradis fiscaux: 16 milliards de dollars d'impots eludes," Chaire d'etudes socioliques, Université du Québec à Montréal, 2008.

24 Sanger, *Fair Shares*, 25.

25 Dean Baker and Travis MacArthur, *The Value of the "Too Big to Fail" Big Bank Subsidy*, Centre for Economic and Policy Research, September 2009, www.cepr.net/documents/publications/too-big-to-fail-2009-09.pdf.

26 Sanger, *Fair Shares*, 11.

27 Janice Atkinson-Small, "Cameron Must Stand Up Against the EU Tax That Could Destroy Our Finance Industry," *Mail Online*, October 31, 2011, www.dailymail.co.uk/debate/article-2055634/A-financial-transactions-tax-disaster-Britain.html.

28 European Commission 2012. "Technical Fiche: Tax Collection," ec.europa.eu/taxation_customs/resources/documents/taxation/other_taxes/financial_sector/fact_sheet/tax-collection.pdf.

29 Christopher L. Culp, "Financial Transaction Taxes: Benefits and Costs," Compass Lexecon, March 16, 2010, www.rmcsinc.com/articles/FTTCLC.pdf.

30 This was recently noted in *The Economist*, "Beyond Bretton Woods 2," November 4, 2010, 85, www.ist.com/node/17414511; and a decade earlier by Joseph Stiglitz, "Must Financial Crises Be This Frequent and This Painful?", *Policy Options*, July 1999, www.irpp.org/po/archive/jul99/stiglitz.pdf.

31 John Lipsky, "Economic Shifts and Oil Price Volatility," presentation by Lipsky, First Deputy Managing Director, International Monetary Fund, at the 4th OPEC International Seminar Vienna, March 18, 2009, www.imf.org/external/np/speeches/2009/031809.htm; Ben Bernanke, "The Great Moderation," remarks at meetings of the Eastern Economics Association, Washington, D.C., February 20, 2004, www.federalreserve.gov/BOARDDOCS/SPEECHES/2004/20040220/default.htm.

32 Eric Lascelles, "Ever More Bubbles, Ever More Quickly? Market Musings," TD Securities, November 25, 2009.

33 Stamp out Poverty, "Financial Transaction Tax: Myth Busting," April 2012, www.stampoutpoverty.org/?lid=11539.

34 Gordon Edall, "Upstart Exchanges Complicate Stock Pricing," *Globe and Mail*,

February 9, 2010, www.theglobeandmail.com/globe-investor/investment-ideas/ number-cruncher/upstart-exchanges-complicate-stock-pricing/article1462024.

35 Jim Flaherty, "The Eurozone Should Sort Out Its Own Mess," *The Telegraph,* May 1, 2012, www.telegraph.co.uk/finance/financialcrisis/9238854/The-eurozone-should-sort-out-its-own-mess.html.

36 "JPMorgan's Trading Loss Is Said to Rise at Least 50%." *New York Times,* May 16, 2012, dealbook.nytimes.com/2012/05/16/jpmorgans-trading-loss-is-said-to-rise-at-least-50.

7 Taxes and Ecological Justice?

1 www.monbiot.com/2009/12/01/the-urgent-threat-to-world-peace-is-%E2%80%A6-canada.

2 www.adbusters.org/magazine/102/canadas-hard-right-turn.html.

3 blackoutspeakout.ca.

4 www.thestar.com/news/article/176382-harper-letter-called-kyoto-socialist-scheme.

5 www.thestar.com/news/canada/article/892053-climate-bill-commons-crushed-in-one-blow.

6 www.budget.gc.ca/2012/rd-dc/speech-discours-eng.html.

7 nrtee-trnee.ca/reality-check-the-state-of-climate-progress-in-canada.

8 For insights on this section, the author thanks David Thompson at www.sustainableprosperity.ca.

9 www.canadainternational.gc.ca/g20/summit-sommet/g20/declaration_092509 .aspx?view=d, #24.

10 www.windsorstar.com/technology/Canada+shielding+fossil+fuel+subsidies+Earth+Summit/6794291/story.html.

11 For insights on this section, the author thanks Daniela Ljomov.

12 Tim Flannery, *The Weather Makers: How We Are Changing the Climate and What It Means for Life on Earth* (New York, HarperCollins, 2005), 170.

13 David Suzuki Foundation, "Industry Solutions," www.davidsuzuki.org/issues/ climate-change/science/climate-solutions/industry-solutions.

14 The term "carbon pricing" or "carbon tax" is used because carbon dioxide, an end product of the burning of carbon-containing fossil fuels, is the principle contributor to GHG pollution. However, carbon pricing can also be applied to activities that release other GHGs, such as methane (landfill waste sites, agriculture) and nitrous oxide (chemical fertilizers). Pembina Institute and David Suzuki Foundation, "Carbon Taxes: Key Issues, Key Questions," May 29, 2008, pubs.pembina.org/ reports/carbontaxfactsheetv2.pdf, 1.

15 Sustainable Prosperity, "Policy Brief: Carbon Pricing, Investment and the Low Car-

bon Economy" June 2010, www.sustainableprosperity.ca/article168&highlight=
carbon%20pricing,%20investment%20and%20a%20low%20carbon%20economy.

16 Carbon Tax Centre, "Introduction," March 3, 2010,
    www.carbontax.org/introduction.

17 Matt Horne, "Putting a Price on Pollution," Pembina Institute, March 3, 2010,
    www.pembina.org/op-ed/2006.

18 British Columbia Ministry of Finance, "How the Carbon Tax Works,"
    www.fin.gov.bc.ca/tbs/tp/climate/A4.htm.

19 Ontario Ministry of the Environment, "Participating in Cap and Trade," January 24,
    2011,   www.ene.gov.on.ca/environment/en/category/climate_change/STDPROD_
    078899#trade.

20 Pembina Institute and David Suzuki Foundation, "Carbon Taxes: Key Issues, Key
    Questions," 2.

21 Carbon Tax Center, "Tax vs. Cap-Trade," May 12, 2009, www.carbontax.org/issues/
    carbon-taxes-vs-cap-and-trade.

22 Pembina Institute and David Suzuki Foundation, "Carbon Taxes: Key Issues, Key
    Questions," 2.

23 www.gouv.qc.ca/portail/quebec/international/general/quebec/grand_dossiers/
    climat/?lang=en.

24 CTV News Montreal, "Quebec Imposes Carbon Tax on Energy Producers," June 7,
    2007,   toronto.ctv.ca/servlet/an/local/CTVNews/20070607/quebec_carbontax_
    070607?hub=MontrealHome.

25 www.mddep.gouv.qc.ca/changements/plan_action/index-en.htm.

26 Matt Horne, *Pembina Recommends Ways to Strengthen B.C.'s Carbon Tax*, Pem-
    bina Institute, January 28, 2010, www.pembina.org/media-release/1962.

27 British Columbia Ministry of Finance, "Budget and Fiscal Plan 2008/2009–
    2010/2011," February 19, 2008,
    www.bcbudget.gov.bc.ca/2008/bfp/2008_Budget_Fiscal_Plan.pdf, 12.

28 British Columbia Ministry of Finance, "How the Carbon Tax Works,"
    www.fin.gov.bc.ca/tbs/tp/climate/A4.htm.

29 B.C. Ministry of Finance, "Budget and Fiscal Plan 2008/2009–2010/2011," 1.

30 Western Climate Initiative, "Clean Energy: Creating Jobs, Protecting the Environ-
    ment," brochure, May, 2010, 3.

31 The WCI cap-and-trade system will cover carbon dioxide, methane, nitrous oxide,
    hydrofluorocarbons, perfluorocarbons, sulfur hexafluoride, and nitrogen trifluoride
    emissions. Western Climate Initiative, "The WCI Cap and Trade Program," 2010,
    www.westernclimateinitiative.org/the-wci-cap-and-trade-program.

32 Ibid.

33 European Commission Climate Action, "Emissions Trading System Policy,"

November 15, 2010, ec.europa.eu/clima/policies/ets/index_en.htm.

34 European Commission Climate Action, "Reducing Emissions from the Aviation Sector," January 4, 2011,
ec.europa.eu/clima/policies/transport/aviation/index_en.htm.

35 EC Climate Action, "Emissions Trading System Policy."

36 www.pwc.com.au/consulting/assets/publications/Carbon-Pricing-Plan-Oct11-Jun12.pdf.

37 Pembina Institute and David Suzuki Foundation, "Climate Leadership, Economic Prosperity: Final Report on an Economic Study of the Greenhouse Gas Targets and Policies for Canada," 2009, pubs.pembina.org/reports/climate-leadership-report-en.pdf, v

38 Canadian Centre for Policy Alternatives, "Getting the Job Done Right: Alternative Federal Budget 2010," www.policyalternatives.ca/sites/default/files/uploads/publications/reports/docs/AFB%202010%20Main%20Budget%20Document_0.pdf, 103.

39 webarchive.nationalarchives.gov.uk/+/www.hm-treasury.gov.uk/sternreview_index.htm.

40 www.un.org/en/development/desa/policy/wess/wess_current/2012wesspr_en.pdf.

41 pubs.pembina.org/reports/eco-survey-2011-eng-final.pdf.

42 www.hilltimes.com/news/politics/2012/07/04/%E2%80%98we-were-kind-of-the-last-man-standing%E2%80%99-outgoing-nrtee-president-defends-its/31354.

43 www.greenbudget.ca/main_e.html.

44 Stéphane Dion and Éloi Laurent, "From Rio to Rio: A Global Carbon Price Signal to Escape the Great Climate Inconsistency," www.ofce.sciences-po.fr/pdf/dtravail/WP2012-16.pdf.

45 www.policyalternatives.ca/sites/default/files/uploads/publications/National%20Office/2012/03/AFB2012%20Budget%20Document.pdf.

46 canada2020.ca/canada-we-want/wp-content/themes/canada2020/assets/pdf/en/Canada2020_English_Carbon-4.pdf, 63.

47 Stewart Elgie and Alex Wood, ibid, page 89.

48 Van Jones, *The Green Collar Economy: How One Solution Can Fix Our Two Biggest Problems* (New York: HarperCollins, 2008).

49 www.policyalternatives.ca/publications/reports/who-occupies-sky; www.cpj.ca/files/docs/CPJ_position_statement.pdf.

8 Tax Justice and the Civil Economy

1 Statistics Canada survey findings in 1997, 2000, and 2003.

2 V. Zamagni, "Italy's Cooperatives from Marginality to Success," paper presented at 14th International Economic History Congress, Helsinki, August 21–25, 2008.

3 R. Lotti, R., P. Mensing, and D. Valenti, "A Co-operative Solution: This Self-Governing Corporate Structure Protects Communities and Prospers in a Globalizing World," *Management Quarterly* 47, no. 3 (Fall 2006): 8.

4 Presentation to class in Bologna Summer Program, 2007.

5 M.J. Adeler, "Enabling Environments for Co-operative Development – A Comparative Experience," Centre for the Study of Co-operatives, University of Saskatchewan Institute of Urban Studies, and University of Winnipeg, 2009.

6 J. Logue, *Economics, Cooperation, and Employee Ownership: The Emilia Romagna Model – in More Detail* (Kent: Ohio Employee Ownership Center, 2006).

7 A great deal has recently been written on social capital, but see in particular Robert Putnam.

8 Logue, *Economics, Cooperation, and Employee Ownership.*

9 A. Cooper, "Basque Region Stands Strong Despite Shaky Spain," Reuters, June 28, 2012.

10 G. MacLeod, *From Mondragon to America: Experiences in Community Economic Development* (Sidney: University College of Cape Breton Press, 1997); M. Lutz, "The Mondragon Co-operative Complex: An Application of Kantian Ethics to Social Economics." *International Journal of Social Economics* 24, no. 12 (1997).

11 Ibid., 5.

12 Ibid., 5.

13 Ibid.

14 D. Côté, "Best Practices and Co-operative Development in Quebec," in *Effective Practices in Starting Co-ops: The Voice of Canadian Co-op Developers,* ed. J. Emmanuel and L. Cayo (Victoria: New Rochdale Press, 2007; and B.C. Institute for Co-operative Studies, University of Victoria).

15 L. Labelle, "Development of Cooperatives and Employee Ownership, Quebec Style" (1999), cog.kent.edu/lib/Labelle.htm.

16 On Co-op Blog, "Survival Rate of Co-operatives in Quebec," Quebec Ministry of Economic Development, Innovation and Export, 2008, ontariocoops.wordpress.com/reports/survival-rate-of-co-operatives-in-quebec-2008.

17 A speech by Vaclav Havel, President of the Czech Republic, on the occasion of "Vaclav Havel's Civil Society Symposium," Macalester College, St. Paul, April 26, 1999.

18 N. Gilbert and P. Terrell, *Dimensions of Social Welfare Policy* (Toronto: Allyn & Bacon, 2005).

Contributors

James Clancy is the National President of the 340,000-member National Union of Public and General Employees (NUPGE).

Dennis Howlett is the Executive Director of Canadians for Tax Fairness.

Trish Hennessy is the founding director of the new Ontario office of the Canadian Centre for Policy Alternatives. She also founded and directed the CCPA's national project examining income inequality. Visit her blog at www.frameincanada.com.

Diana Gibson has worked nationally and internationally on economic and public policy issues ranging from health care and inequality to energy and trade policy.

Richard Swift is a freelance journalist and social activist and former editor at the Oxford-based *New Internationalist* magazine.

Peter Gillespie works with the Ottawa-based Halifax Initiative, a Canadian coalition of development, environment, faith-based, human rights, and labour organizations concerned with economic justice.

Jim Stanford is an economist with the Canadian Auto Workers and author of *Economics for Everyone* (Halifax: Fernwood, and the Canadian Centre for Policy Alternatives).

Toby Sanger works as the economist for the Canadian Union of Public Employees.

Joe Gunn is the Ottawa-based executive director of Citizens for Public Justice, www.cpj.ca, an organization that promotes justice, peace, and the integrity of creation. He also serves on the Board of Canadians for Tax Fairness.

John Restakis is Executive Director of the B.C. Co-operative Association.

Murray Dobbin is a veteran writer and activist and President of Canadians for Tax Fairness.